MW01164751

# PRAISE ᵗ
# FINDING GOD IN SUFFERING

Richly textured with biblical, theological, and pastoral insights, this volume—one of Epperly's finest—challenges age-old assumptions that not only added to Job's woes, but still remain entrenched in modern thinking. *Journey with Job* is a wise, honest, and liberating approach to one of the most difficult questions we face.

**Patricia Adams Farmer**
Author of *Embracing a Beautiful God*

In the skillful and insightful hands of Bruce Epperly, Job becomes one of our earliest theologians, raising questions about how we understand God and live out that understanding. Reminding us that Job is designed to counter theologies that blame the victim and promise more than they can deliver, Epperly uses Job to unmask these pretenders and invites us to cast a different vision, in which we can discover God's presence even in the midst of suffering. This slender book should prove to be a blessing to all who are searching for a God whose love is steadfast and liberating.

**Robert Cornwall**
Pastor, Central Woodward Christian Church

I have a love/hate relationship with Job. If I'm reading an insightful exposition, one which highlights the deep, poetic messages of the book, I love Job. If I'm reading a dry commentary drawing traditional conclusions, I want to chuck Job in the round file. Today I love Job again.

Epperly doesn't pull punches, yet his writing is tender and honest. As he explains, reading Job is not for the faint-hearted. It is a theology which emerges from the vantage point of excruciating and undeserved pain. It is written in the place where the rubber meets the road. And it is the experience of every man and woman on earth.

The question of why remains unanswered. Are we really supposed to believe that Job's intense pain is the result of God and Satan sharing a friendly wager? Is God really that amoral, acting no differently than the arbitrary behavior of the surrounding nations' deities?

God's ways are beyond our comprehension. Job's spiritual growth requires stepping out of his comfortable paradigm where the universe is intricately structured, where goodness is always rewarded and evil is always punished, so that he can embrace the unknown and unsolvable ... while retaining an intimacy with God even in times of pain. In this chaos, Job finally finds peace.

Here's an interesting observation by Epperly: "I have found that many people are more reticent to question God's omnipotence, his unrestricted ability to achieve his will, than God's love. They can live with God causing cancer or a devastating earthquake, but worry that a loving God might not be powerful enough to insure that God's will be done..."

Read this one; it's a journey you don't want to miss. You may find yourself losing faith in the God you thought you knew, only to find the living God. Comfort hides in deep waters.

**Lee Harmon**, *The Dubious Disciple*
Author of *The River of Life: Where Liberal and Conservative Christianity Meet*

In a world daily presenting calamities riddled with your own personal suffering, you need a reliable guide. Bruce Epperly takes you to the concentrated point of suffering in the Bible's story of Job, whose friends fire off answers one by one. Epperly leaves you with a God bigger than failed theological boxes and held by a Web of Love inviting you to prayerful practices on your own and together.

**Kent Ira Groff**, Denver, Colorado
Retreat leader, spiritual guide and author of *Honest to God Prayer* and *Clergy Table Talk*

This book takes an honored place on the shelf of Bruce Epperly's large number of published works. The author brings readers to look into the face of suffering, one of life's most difficulty experiences. Using the experience of Job as a lens, Epperly empathetically helps us name the multiple dynamics in experiences of suffering. In dialogue with the theology of the book of Job and the wider family of process theology, the author helps us articulate a way of understanding God's presence in suffering in which God is not responsible for such devastating turns of events, but in which God is ever present, ever in solidarity, and ever in support in love. Written in touch with deep human experience, in pastoral theological tone, and with clarity, this book is an excellent resource for individual reading and for group discussion. As a preacher, I have to note that it has many passages that will make their way into sermons in the coming years.

**Ronald J. Allen**
Professor of Preaching and Gospels and Letters,
Christian Theological Seminary

# FINDING GOD IN SUFFERING

## A JOURNEY WITH JOB

BRUCE G. EPPERLY

Energion Publications
Gonzalez, FL
2014

ISBN10: 1-63199-107-8
ISBN13: 978-1-63199-107-3
Library of Congress Control Number: 2014957828

Energion Publications
P. O. Box 841
Gonzalez, FL 32560
850-525-3916

energionpubs.com
pubs@energion.com

# TABLE OF CONTENTS

# A Word for the Journey

Over thirty years ago, my pastor-mentor George Tolman, Senior Pastor of First Christian Church in Tucson, Arizona, stated in a sermon, "life is risky business, no one gets out alive, and on the way, there's plenty of pain as well as joy." The author and main character of Job would agree with this sentiment. As a pastor for nearly thirty five years, I've experienced the pain and grief occasioned by serious illness, the dying process, and the loss of loved ones. I've struggled with persons dealing with addictions, job loss, divorce, depression, unexpected catastrophic accidents, and financial and professional failure. Often there appears to be no hope for healing and recovery, and we walk together not knowing where to find a path toward wholeness and unsure of the final outcome of our journey. Explicitly or implicitly, questions of God and the meaning of life, as well as our role in the pain we and our loved ones experience emerge. A pastor's role is to be a companion on the journey, rather than the source of clear and concise answers, as we seek healing in challenging situations. A pastor's calling is to be present and remain open-hearted to others' pain and distress.

It has been said that theology begins in the experience of suffering. At the very least, debilitating suffering challenges our images of success and security, and invites us on a quest for something solid and dependable when the foundations of our lives are shaking. The book of Job emerges from one person's unexpected encounter with suffering. Job seeks God's presence, and to find a God he can trust again, he must jettison his previous images of God. He must let go of his image of an intricately structured universe, in which goodness is always rewarded and evil always punished proportionate to our behavior. On the way, he loses faith in his tradition's image of God, and begins to discover a vision of God large enough to embrace the unknown and unsolvable, and yet intimate enough to be a source of comfort and insight in time of pain.

As pastor-theologian, it is my calling to be a pilgrim with those who suffer, and to reflect on the meaning of suffering, and God's presence in the pain we experience, often for no apparent reason and no fault of our own. In this spirit, I am grateful for the opportunity to share my insights based on a course "Experiencing God in Suffering: A Journey with Job," held at South Congregational Church, United Church of Christ, in Centerville, Massachusetts. Amid the beauty of Cape Cod, just a few minutes' walk from the seashore, our study groups reflected on the very real pain that people experience. We pondered the text of Job and also the textbook of our lives seeking insight into God's presence in times of pain and failure. Every member of the groups had faced serious illness, was experiencing diminishments of the aging process, or lived with the loss of loved ones. I am grateful to my Sunday and Tuesday morning groups for their commitment, insight, and contribution to this text. Although this text emerged from my reflections and reflects my vision of Job and the challenges of suffering, it was profoundly shaped by our weekly conversations.

I am grateful to the members of South Congregational Church, the Job study groups, and persons over the past thirty five years who have come to me with questions and struggles. Their experiences inspired me to explore the problem of evil and the reality of suffering through the lens of the Book of Job. They also helped me discover healthy and supportive ways to respond to my own and my congregants' suffering. Pastors and helpful friends, as the text of Job reveals, can do much harm to people who suffer, especially when they blame the victim, minimize peoples' pain, or provide superficial solutions.

I dedicate this text to my mother-in-law Maxine Gould, who faced her own death this year with grace and equanimity, to my son Matt, a cancer survivor, and all my dear companions facing life-threatening illness. My prayer is that every reader experiences a sense of divine companionship and inspiration amid the inevitable pain and loss that comes with the tragic beauty of human life.

The Season of Pentecost 2014

# Theology For Those Who Suffer

**M**ary called me in a state of shock.[1] We had been friends since high school, and because she knew I was a pastor, she often confided in me during difficult times. "I don't know how to say this, and almost can't get the words out, but I just got the results of the scan. I have incurable cancer and may have less than a year to live. How can this be happening to me? I'm finally happy with my professional life and just got engaged, and my kids still need a mother!" Several months later, I received the news of Mary's death.

Alex was visibly upset when he came to my study. His world had fallen apart with virtually no warning. In the course of a week, his wife told him that she wanted a divorce and he received word that his position would be eliminated. He shared his disbelief and frustration at this unexpected and undeserved turn of events. "I've done everything the way I was taught. I was a faithful husband, good breadwinner, and caring father. I devoted thirty years to the company and only missed two day's work. I went beyond the call of duty, and now it's all falling apart. All my life, I've been told that if you work hard and support your family, everything will be alright. And, now this! Am I being punished for something I don't know? What's God trying to tell me? Did I do something wrong?"

Susan had been a dedicated congregant at a local Pentecostal church. For most of her adult life, she believed that God rewarded the righteous and punished sinners in this lifetime and the next. She took seriously the words of her pastor and the televangelists,

---

1   I have chosen pseudonyms to affirm the privacy of persons mentioned in this text.

whose sermons counseled that if you plant a seed of faith by giving generously to your church and their television ministries, God will bless you with good health, financial prosperity, and a happy home life. But, now, as she surveyed her life, she saw nothing but chaos: financial insecurity and a possible home foreclosure, kids doing drugs, and constant physical pain from arthritis. Her faith was also in chaos. "I did the right things. I followed God's way and gave to the church above and beyond our financial ability. I trusted that God would bless us. Is God punishing me? Or, is God testing my faith? Is this all just a hoax to fill the collection plates and build a television empire? Right now, I don't know what to believe. Was I just a sucker, the victim of some kind of spiritual pyramid scheme? Was the promise of prosperity a hoax? I don't know if I can believe in God anymore!"

As I write these words, people in nearby Boston are remembering last year's Boston Marathon bombings, a mudslide recently leveled a town in the Pacific Northwest, a truck crossed a divider killing teenagers on a college tour, a plane has been lost at sea, and another school child has been the victim of gun violence. Each of these victims, and their families, began their day thinking they were safe and believing that life would go on without any significant interruptions. Without warning and for no apparent reason, life collapsed for them and their loved ones. The world is a risky place, whether as a result human decision-making, acts of violence and corporate decision-making, mechanical failures, and natural catastrophes, often inaccurately described as "acts of God." Moreover, sometimes "stuff happens," and life appears to be random in its bestowal of blessing and misfortune. At such moments, we look for a reason why some die and others flourish; why some rise to the top and others fail; why the tornado struck here and not down the road; or why an innocent child must suffer pain and disability, while another child runs happily home from school.

For many people, even those who would describe themselves as agnostics, the question of God emerges at times of unanticipated and apparently unwarranted encounters with death and destruction. "God, why did you do this to me? What good can come from punishing my child with a devastating illness? Do you care at all about the pain we feel or are we pawns in some sort of cosmic chess game?"

Philosopher Alfred North Whitehead once stated that philosophy could be seen as a series of footnotes to Plato, who raised most of the important philosophical questions in Western thought. The same could be said for Job in terms of the problem of evil, or theodicy, and our responses to the sufferings of ourselves and others. In a manner unexcelled in insight for over twenty five hundred years, the book of Job raises questions about the origin and reality of suffering, starkly and without denial. The author of Job asserts without equivocation that suffering is real and that personal and corporate disaster can strike at any time, without notice, and turn our theological and spiritual worlds upside down. Reading the book of Job is not for the faint-hearted or those who want easy answers to life's greatest questions.

Readers of Job may discover that there are no clear answers to the origin and reality of suffering. Still, the author of Job invites all of us to live in solidarity with those who suffer. The book of Job reminds us that regardless of our piety, economic, or spiritual achievements, no one is immune from the sufferings of body, mind, and spirit felt by a man named Job.

## Theology Where the Pain Is

It has been said that theology begins in the experience of suffering and disappointment. If this description of the origins of theology is accurate, then Job is one of the greatest theological texts. The book of Job is not theology written from the armchair and delivered to a self-satisfied and comfortable audience, but theology that emerges from the vantage point of excruciating and undeserved pain. Job is practical and pastoral in nature. It is written at the place where the rubber meets the road; Job makes his complaint from the perspective of an ash heap after having lost everything that characterized his once enviable life - wealth, social position, family, and personal health. Job even has lost his faith in the God of his religious tradition, whom he and his friends believed rewarded the righteous, punished evil doers, and insured an orderly and predictable universe. Job believes in God, but he is now uncertain about God's nature and attitude toward humankind.

The book of Job is our story. Job's wisdom enlightens our experiences in the emergency room terrified by chest pains and shortness of breath; in the Alzheimer's wing grieving when a beloved companion no longer recognizes us and treats another patient as if he or she were their spouse; at our child's evaluation for autism; and at the bedside and graveside of a parent or companion. Job's wisdom touches the grief and despair of parents of children who have gone missing or been kidnapped by terrorist groups. Job speaks to those whose lives have been turned upside down by earthquake, hurricane, flood, and cyclone.

The book of Job invites us to claim our identity as theologians. Job shouts out to us, "You are a theologian" because we have experienced the pain of the world and are trying to make sense of it. Job shouts to us: "Don't let the word 'theology' put you off. By whatever word, we strive to make sense of the senseless and meaning of the meaningless." We become theologians the moment we begin to ask hard questions about life and the One who creates the universe and gives birth to each moment of experience. Theology asks questions of life, death, meaning, human hope, and immortality. It also raises questions about the meaning and purpose of our brief, and often challenging and ambiguous lives. For Job, theology and spirituality are intimately related. As Episcopalian spiritual guide Alan Jones once asserted, spirituality deals with the unfixable aspects of life – or what I would describe as life's inevitabilities. Sooner or later even the most fortunate of us must make theological and personal sense of what is beyond our control, while taking responsibility for what we can change.

Once upon a time, a seeker from another religion, the Indian Prince Gautama was faced with the problem of evil. He had been sheltered from suffering until young adulthood until, over the course of three days, he observed three realities that had been hidden by the protective walls of his father's palace: an elderly person, a sick person, and a corpse. He realized that our attitude toward life is the source of suffering, and that only a life committed to spiritual practice can liberate us from the pain and suffering brought on by the interplay of desire, change, and mortality. From his reflections, one of the world's great wisdom traditions, Buddhism, was born.

Whether we look at the world from the vantage point of Buddha or Job, or from East or West, theological reflection invites us to ask questions about what is most important to us in life and how we can experience joy and equanimity in the midst of what Judith Viorst described as life's necessary losses. Theological reflection reminds us that what we believe about God and ourselves is important. Our beliefs can cure or kill. They can provide comfort or traumatize. The book of Job also cautions us that theological counsel, especially by ministers and religious leaders, should fall under the guidance of the Hippocratic Oath, "first do no harm."

Just think of the thoughtless theological speculation publically voiced by popular religious leaders, who have asserted that:

- The terrorist attacks of 9/11 resulted from God's withdrawing divine protection on the United States as a result of its immorality.
- The devastating impact of Hurricane Katrina on New Orleans was divine punishment for the city's tolerance of homosexuality.
- The Haiti earthquake was the result of a pact with the devil to gain freedom from European rule in the 19th century.
- AIDS was God's punishment of the United States for its turning away from traditional Christian values.

While these statements claim to reflect orthodox biblical perspectives, can you imagine how these statements would be heard by the child of one of the victims of 9/11, a family who lost its home and livelihood from Katrina, or the parent of a child, dying of AIDS due to a blood transfusion? If theology begins where the pain is, then we have to ask, "How is our theology experienced by those whose lives have been devastated for no apparent reason and without warning? How would these proclamations respond to the pain of a family whose four year old has been kidnapped or diagnosed with cancer? How would a child receiving chemotherapy understand the God who has supposedly punished him with cancer?" Some people excuse or praise behaviors by God that would lead to incarceration if performed by humans!

A few weeks ago, as I switched from channel to channel looking for a bit of diversion amid the rigors of pastoral ministry during Holy Week, I came upon a proponent of the contemporary prosperity gospel, who challenged his television audience to "just plant a seed of faith and prepare for your great harvest." Viewers were given the opportunity to plant spiritual seeds with Master Card or Visa! I couldn't help but pause to reflect on how many seeds wither and how many assurances of prosperity and success fail to come true, despite the televangelist's promises. In what ways do these promises end up spiritually harming vulnerable and economically insecure people? While I believe that our faith activates and opens us to new possibilities, our faith does not guarantee a particular outcome or happy ending to every story.

In light of easy and glib responses to the problem of suffering, the book of Job is a type of theological Lysol, eliminating the spiritual sepsis of certain theological explanations and pastoral responses to suffering and pain. Job challenges us, first of all, to be pastoral in responding to the needs of others and, then, to articulate explanations of suffering, worthy of the God we worship. While Job might not fully agree with Albert Einstein's musings on the reality of chaos and suffering, he would have recognized wisdom in the questions Einstein raises:

- Does God play dice?
- Is the universe friendly?

The Book of Job doesn't give us a solution to life's sufferings, but he poses the right questions to guide us in our quest to experience God in the midst of suffering.

## Reading Job

Reading Job takes you into the world of Shakespeare's plays and Plato's dialogues or a postmodern novel or film. The book of Job presents a variety of voices, raises numerous questions, and provides no clear resolutions to life's problems. It's as if they remind us that the problem of suffering can only be solved, and always tentatively, by walking through our own pain and the pain of others with an open mind and a compassionate heart.

The author of Job is a wisdom teacher, who searches for God in the joys and sorrows of daily life. There is no easily understandable divine plan, nor can we fully discern God's purposes from our finite perspective. Job's author is unconcerned with God's deliverance of the Israelites from captivity or God's continuing activity in Israel's history. This high mark of wisdom literature is no "purpose driven" spiritual guidebook to solving the problem of evil but an "adventure of ideas," in which no voices are excluded and no possibilities eliminated. Everything we thought was stable and all the creeds we lived by are on the table, including our beliefs about God. The author of Job recognizes that fidelity to God is not found in the recitation of instant answers but in wrestling with God, like Jacob at the stream of Jabbok in search of a blessing. Chapters three to thirty seven of the book of Job read like a theological tennis match, gaining in intensity with each volley and occasionally collapsing into chaos as if all the contestants are shouting at once.

Reading Job may not give us the "right" answers, but it steers us away from theological and spiritual platitudes that ultimately do more harm than good to those who suffer. Amid the many voices of Job, there is an underlying call to listen to the voices of suffering, our own and others, with our whole hearts. As we will see, when we silence the voices of pain or provide easy explanations, we end up minimizing peoples' pain and blaming them for their condition. In contrast to theologies than deny or minimize the pain of others, we must, in the spirit of the healer Jesus, respond to peoples' pain with words and acts of healing regardless of who is at fault.

## Talking About God

Old Testament scholar Terence Fretheim once noted that the most important theological question is not "Do you believe in God?" but "What kind of God do you believe in?" The author of Job would concur with Fretheim's vision. Job is a God-filled book, reflecting the deep piety of its author and his main character. Like the Psalms, Job describes a faith for every season of life and shows that piety can be revealed as much in our questions as in our affirmations.

The author of Job and his protagonist are serious men. Job, the author and character, takes seriously the consequences of sin and the wondrous insecurity of life. There are few "praise the Lords" in Job, but a deep faith tempered by the realities of suffering and silence. Job never gives up on God, despite God's apparent absence. The intensity of Job's protest gives witness to the importance of his quest to find a vision of God worth believing. Job's previous understandings of God have proven inadequate in light of Job's suffering. Yesterday's easily-recited orthodoxies no longer fit Job's lived experience. He needs to discover a vision of God expansive enough to embrace what the philosopher Whitehead describes as the tragic beauty of life.

Over two thousand years later, German-American theologian Paul Tillich spoke of faith as involving our "ultimate concern," what is most important to us, and asserted that the experience of doubt is essential to deep faith. Tillich believed that we can claim certainty about our experience of the Holy and its impact on our lives, while struggling with doubts about the nature and character of what is most important to us. Job would agree. He believes in God, but is in search of a God whom he can trust when life collapses around him. The orthodox God, who rewards and punishes us according to our behavior, has died. What vision of God will emerge out of the chaos of suffering and abandonment? We can only seek and hope to find!

Job's struggle to find a God he can believe in is reflected in the dynamic and necessary tension between the *apophatic* and *kata-*

*phatic* approaches to God. The *kataphatic* (in Greek, "with images") approach treasures our experiences of God and the words we use to describe our relationship with the Creator. We sing praises to God, describing God as friend, companion, healer, and rock of ages. We create creeds and holy books to portray God's nature and relationship with humankind. Worship demands that we articulate words and images for God. Still, we must be careful in our descriptions of the Holy One in order to avoid localizing God's presence to one place, culture, or religious tradition. One of the problems with Job's friends' orthodox theological affirmations is that they claim to know too much about God. Like Aslan, the Christ-lion of C.S. Lewis' *Chronicles of Narnia*, God is not "tame," nor can God's nature be limited by human language, worship, or doctrine. Believing they have figured God out and banishing mystery from their religion, they have little sympathy with Job's experience and assume his suffering can easily be explained as punishment for his sins.

The *apophatic* (in Greek, "without images") approach serves as a type of "theological Lysol," eliminating the germs of theological pretense and reminding us of our mortality, error, finitude, and sin. God is more than we can image, the *apophatic* path asserts. When God speaks out of the whirlwind, God shows Job the wondrous beauty and complexity of the universe. Job is overwhelmed and confesses that his quest to fully define God's ways is misguided. God is more than we can imagine, whether in Job's mystic vision or in the descriptions of today's cosmologists who imagine a 125 billion galaxy, 13.8 billion year old, cosmic adventure, and then remind us that our beautiful earth is just a speck in our home galaxy, the Milky Way.

The book of Job testifies to the importance of faithful agnosticism: if we think we can know God or God's ways fully, we have created an idol of our own making, subject to our cultural norms and ethics. Still, in a spirit similar to the Greek sage Socrates, Job reminds us that, at the very least, we are obligated to challenge harmful and parochial images of God. The book of Job's many voices provide us with a deeply faithful agnosticism in which we devote our lives to a Reality that is always more than we can imagine. The adventure of faith is always on the move, always growing by trial and error. It always stays honest and healthy through the humble recognition of our limitations and the impact of our community's finite and biased perspectives on our understanding of the Holy One. Faithful Job will test his own faith and challenge the God he once believed in, looking for an answer that goes far beyond the certainties of his religious tradition. He risks losing his religion, but in the process he may discover the living God.

## Journeying With Job

Each chapter ends with a simple spiritual practice and a few questions for reflection. As I have written elsewhere, I believe that holistic theological reflection involves the interplay of vision and practice. Our personal or community vision is our tentative and humble understanding of the universe and our place in it. Our vision can be described as our theological perspective and involves our images of God, human life, the cosmos, our vocation, the meaning of suffering, and survival after death. Though some persons seek unchanging absolutes, a healthy vision is always on the move, open to growth and new insights, grounded in the recognition that every belief system and faith tradition is finite, time-bound, and reflective of certain perspectives on God and the world. Spiritual practice involves ways that help us experience life in its depths and discover God's presence in life's joys and challenges. Practices open our hearts and connect us with the wellsprings of God's healing energy. Practices are not ways to avoid pain or deny our suffering and the suffering of the world, but pathways to gracefully and courageously face the deepest realities of life, including death, diminishment, grief, loss, and beauty.

In our first spiritual practice, take a few minutes to pause and gently breathe. Imagine that each breath opens you to God's Spirit moving through your life. After you experience a sense of calm, take a few minutes for a life review, considering the following questions:

1) What is your first recollection of the world as a place of pain as well as joy? What event awakened you to the pain of the world? How did the people around you, especially adults, react to that event?

2) What has been the most devastating experience in your life? What was most difficult about that experience? How did you respond to that experience? What helped you make it through this experience?

3) Where have you experienced God's presence in moments of suffering?

Conclude this time of reflection with a prayer that your heart might open with compassion toward your suffering and the suffering of the world.

## Questions For Reflection

1) Do you think religious faith guarantees well-being and success? How do you respond to the three stories with which the chapter begins? In what ways might faith improve your life? Are there any limits to the impact of our faith on our life situation?

2) How do you explain the evils of the world? What are the sources of the suffering we experience?

3) A prominent religious figure stated the following: "The impact of Hurricane Katrina on New Orleans was divine punishment for the city's tolerance of homosexuality." How do you evaluate this statement? Does it reflect your understanding of God?

4) Old Testament scholar Terrence Fretheim once noted that the most important theological question is not "Do you believe in God?" but "What kind of God do you believe in?" What do you think of his assertion? Can our images of God be harmful to ourselves and others?

5) Do you think that faith and doubt can coexist in a person's experience of God? Is doubt always a bad thing in the life of faith?

6) In what ways is the apophatic, negative, approach to understanding God helpful? Why is it important to recognize that there are limits to what we can know about God?

7) What images of God give you comfort? What images of God are problematic to you?

# ONCE UPON A TIME IN THE LAND OF UZ

*In preparation, read Job 1:1-2:10*

> *There was one a man in the land of Uz whose name was Job. That man was blameless and upright, one who feared God and turned away from evil.* (Job 1:1)

With this short description, one of the greatest texts of spiritual literature begins. There is no mention of the author, the date of composition, or the intended audience. We don't know Job's ethnicity, religion, or date of birth. Scholars believe that Job is not Jewish, either in faith or ethnicity. In this ethnic and religious vagueness, there is virtue. We soon discover that Job is everyone who has dealt with unexpected tragedy for no apparent reason. Job is everyman and every woman who faces unimaginable suffering and reflects on the origins of her or his pain, and the role of God in determining the affairs of our lives.

The land of Uz is also a mystery as are the locations of Job's friends' homes. Uz is nowhere, and everywhere. Uz is the place we live our lives, raise our families, and face both the joys and tragedies of life. Scholars believe that the biblical book of Job may find its origins in Middle Eastern tales of righteous persons who experience undeserved suffering. The unknown author of Job may be adapting an ancient legend as a vehicle for exploring the reality of suffering in our lives. Job's author doesn't show his cards. He shares many voices and explores many theological pathways and leaves us room to discern God's presence in the pain we experience.

He has one clear position: the acts-consequences view of success and failure and health and disease is not adequate to explain the reality of suffering in human life. He is challenging the received, indeed, scriptural wisdom of his time that asserted the righteous people prosper and unrighteous people fail, whether in terms of economics, relationships, or health.

We don't know exactly when Job was written, though it is often dated between 600 and 300 BCE. We don't know the audience to whom it was written, but suspect it was written to the Jewish people as a theological alterative to Deuteronomy's rewards-punishments understanding of our relationship to God and our own well-being. It might have been written as a way of interpreting the fall of the Northern and Southern Kingdoms of Israel to Babylon and Assyria respectively.

Job is considered wisdom literature in so far as it seeks to discern the presence of God in the global reach of history as well as the minute details of our own lives. There is nothing in Job about "salvation history," God's mighty acts to liberate the Hebrews from captivity in Egypt and lead them to the Promised Land of Israel. We hear nothing about the Jerusalem Temple, the great King David, the prophetic challenge to Israel's neglect of the authentic worship and care for the poor, or any particular commandments required to insure God's favor. Job is a word to all of us who must eventually suffer, either directly in our own skin or through the loss of emotional and economic well-being or through the pain we experience as we helplessly watch as our children, friends, and spouses deal with incurable illness or accidental death. All of us must eventually deal with what can't be avoided, fixed, or healed. Job guides us in our attempt to understand and respond to what defies our hopes and expectations of life.

## A Strange Beginning

The book of Job begins and ends with descriptive prose. The majority of the text is a wildly poetic, and occasionally chaotic, theological tennis match with no clear outcome or victor.

Job begins in Uz, with a description of Job's righteousness, social position, and prosperity. He has wealth, power, and lovely children. He is the envy all who know him. But, in the background, there is always the threat that chaos will be unleashed in the tightly woven fabric of Job's moral universe. Recognizing the moral limitations of his children and eager to protect them from any deserved punishment, according to Job's acts-consequences world view, Job constantly performs sacrifices on their behalf. As Job himself admits, "It may be that my children have sinned, and cursed God in their hearts" (1:5). If somehow a sin passed without atonement, his children's well-being would be jeopardized, as far as this righteous and over-functioning, dare we say co-dependent, parent believed. Job is doing well and his children are flourishing, but tragedy, brought on by divine punishment, can strike at any time if you let your moral and pious guard down.

Job is grateful to God for all of his blessings. But, there is no grace in his relationship to the Creator. Job recognizes that everything he has and his children's well-being is based on pleasing God one action at a time. Blessing is the result of piety and good works; cursing results from infidelity and moral laxity. One mistake, an unacknowledged violation of God's rules, and God will turn on you and your family, and you can lose everything gained from your previous piety. Job implicitly believes that God is exacting, unmerciful, and unbending. There's nothing personal about it. There are rules that must be followed with clear consequences for good and bad behavior, no exceptions.

## A Caucus in Heaven

The scene moves from Uz to heaven, where God has gathered the heavenly beings for a meeting, the purpose of which is unknown to Job and us. God recognizes one of his heavenly assistants, Satan, and inquires about his most recent adventures traveling among humankind. Satan, described in the book of Job, is not the Evil One described in other Jewish and Christian literature. Ha-satan, as he is called, is more like God's eyes and ears on planet Earth.

He observes, takes notes on the behavior of mortals, and looks for faults that may demand punishment. Literally "the accuser," ha-satan serves as a type of divine district attorney or prosecutor, assigned to evaluate our actions and motivations, perhaps as part of the acts-consequences, rewards-punishments understanding of God's relationship to humankind.

What happens next defies our understanding. The Creator of the Universe gets into a brag fest with ha-satan, boasting of Job's fidelity, and then entering into a wager that Job will remain faithful even if he loses everything. Ha-satan suggests that Job is faithful only because of his blessed life and his anticipation that his righteousness will lead to more prosperity in the future. Ha-satan recognizes the weak point in the theology of rewards-punishments. He suggests that Job's faith is a type of barter: Job will be faithful and moral to achieve a good life, defined in terms of health, wealth, social standing, and family life. Ha-satan suggests that if Job loses everything, he will turn from God and become just another amoral mortal. God takes the bait and, as the story goes, lets Satan take everything away from Job except his wife and his life.

The author of Job paints a very dismal picture of God's character and relationship to humankind. The actions of God resemble the arbitrary behavior of the deities of Greek mythology, easily provoked, petty, and unconcerned with human well-being. It is unclear that the author believes that the introductory chapters accurately describe God. But, certainly the God of the first two chapters is less moral than the average human being, and hardly worthy of worship, when placed next to the God who liberates Israel, calls for justice through prophetic voices, or suffers for our salvation on the Cross. At the very least, the God described in Job represents the remorseless amorality of a random universe in which tsunami, flood, and earthquake along with cancer and ALS occur for no reason discernable to those who suffer. In the language of Job's divinity, "you [ha-satan] incited me against him, to destroy him for no reason" (2:3).

Job is not aware of the debate in heaven or any divine purpose in his suffering. His orderly and predictable world is blown to pieces by forces he can neither understand nor control. Job is everyone: the spouse who grieves for her marathon-running companion who drops dead of a heart attack a few minutes after being pronounced in great health at his annual physical; the passenger who for a split second sees her or his life go before his eyes as the plane goes down; the recent retiree, diagnosed with incurable cancer, as he is planning the holiday of a lifetime; the parent who loses her children in a mudslide; and the high school students in shock after a bus accident kills a dozen of their classmates. From our vantage point, there is no reason for death to strike unexpectedly, especially to undeserving victims.

## Hell on Earth

A wager in heaven leads to hell on earth! Job's happy life collapses due to divine decisions undisclosed to Job. Whether the pain we experience is random, God's will, or the result of many factors, much of the time our life is turned upside down without warning or any apparent reason from our standpoint. Pain comes from many sources. Just look at today's paper and you will see pain attributed to natural disasters (floods, tornados, earthquakes, draught); mechanical error or unsafe conditions (airplane crashes, bridge and deck collapses, car crashes); unintentional human error or lack of foresight (the faulty O-ring leading to the Challenger tragedy; a car accident caused by a drowsy driver; failure to fully extinguish a camp fire); bodily causes not attributable to lifestyle or risk factors (certain types of cancer, learning disabilities, ALS, muscular dystrophy); lifestyle (heart disease and certain cancers); and moral lapses or intentional evil actions (accidents caused by alcohol impaired driving, greed leading to the 2008 financial crisis, racist political decisions leading to the Holocaust, the kidnapping of hundreds of girls by a terrorist group in Nigeria). Pain may also be attributed to the confluence of many factors, including personal choices, physical weakness, environmental causes, external stressors, and so on.

In a few short days, Job loses everything. God withdraws his protection of Job, allowing him to become the unwitting victim of both natural and moral evil. Job's life becomes a living hell, physically, spiritually, relationally and economically. He goes from riches to rags, social status to laughing stock, wealth to poverty, and health to sickness. His theological world view, grounded in the dependable order of rewards and punishments collapses as well.

Out of nowhere, on an ordinary day, Sabians steal all of Job's oxen and donkeys and kill his herdsman. Almost simultaneously, an electrical storm, "fire from heaven," kills all of Job's sheep and their caretakers. Shortly thereafter Job receives words that the Chaldeans have stolen all his camels and killed his servants, entrusted with their care. Worse of all, in this perfect storm of destruction, a sheer wind – a sirocco – sweeps across the desert, leveling Job's eldest son's house and killing all his children. Human actions and forces of nature rob Job of everything he holds dear, financially and relationally. The next tragedy comes from within, from the very cells of Job's body. Job is stricken by a physical ailment, a skin disease that makes every movement a misery. Could it have been an ancient form of shingles? Recently, a friend in her mid-fifties was stricken with shingles and was reduced to tears and bedridden by the severity of pain, lasting nearly six weeks. Out of nowhere, without warning, her life became a living hell. Job's devastating losses are the losses everyman and everywoman fear most. Deep down all of us recognize that our lives can be reduced to a living hell if physical illness or economic catastrophe descend upon us without warning or apparent reason. Just the thought of the precarious nature of life sends many of us into temporary moments of anxiety until we regain our – often false - sense of security once more.

## Job Remains Faithful

Job is a person in crisis. He has lost everything. Unknown to him, he is the innocent victim of the arbitrary machinations of a narcissistic God. All Job knows is that the orderly universe he had built his life upon has collapsed into ruins.

Psychiatrist and holocaust survivor Viktor Frankl asserts that they can take away everything from a person except how he/she chooses to respond to the circumstances of life. Equanimity characterizes Job's initial response to losing everything. Tragedy doesn't undermine his piety. Initially, he turns to God in prayer, with awareness that there are no guarantees or entitlements for mortals. He believes that we are creatures of dust who must take life as it comes. God owes us nothing: "Naked I came from my mother's womb, and naked shall I return there; the Lord gave and the Lord has taken away; blessed be the name of the Lord" (1:21). Everything is ultimately God's doing, who bestows upon us bounty or scarcity, joy and sorrow, at God's good pleasure. If I complain at my misfortune, Job initially asserts, I am challenging the divine order of the universe that gives rise to both celebration and tragedy.

Job maintains his spiritual equanimity despite excruciating pain. When Job's wife counsels him to "curse God and die," Job maintains his spiritual resolve, asserting the primacy of God's free will in relationship to humankind: "Shall we receive good at the hand of God, and not receive the bad" (2:10)? Despite the apparent collapse of his rewards-punishments view of reality, Job still upholds the sovereignty of God; all things flow from God's hand and should be received as a gift, regardless of life's circumstances. Acceptance and obedience are the only faithful response to God's sovereign power.

Job's wife receives a bad rap from many readers of the text. Criticized by Job for her snarky comment as a "foolish woman," and never to reappear in the remainder of the book, Job's wife expresses the anger and frustration that will later characterize Job's own attitude toward God's apparent moral mismanagement of the universe. Her bitterness is motivated by love rather than fear or piety. She loves her husband more than she loves God, and enters into battle with anyone, including God, whom she believes is unfairly traumatizing her and her husband. We need to remember that Job's wife has lost everything as well; despite her apparent good health, she has lost her children, economic status, and social standing, and must bear the burden of taking care of a debilitated husband. She is in shock and lashes out at the unfairness of God.

The Letter of James applauds Job's patience (James 5:11). But, Job's patience will come to an end as we move from prose to poetry and dialogue. Still, Job's initial response is one - and not the only – way of responding to the occurrence of tragedy and apparently undeserved suffering. The anger and protest that soon will characterize Job's mood can be equally faithful. Even when Job threatens to file a lawsuit against God, he still remains in communication with the One who appears absent and unfaithful to him. Job's initial patience and equanimity are laudable, but perhaps more laudable is his willingness to share his whole life with God, both praise and provocation.

## Journeying with Job

The precariousness of life can fill us with dread. It can also invite us to treasure each moment, knowing that life is precious and can be taken for granted. For this spiritual practice, take a few minutes, first, for silent prayer, awakening to your quiet center through gentle breathing, inhaling and exhaling the gifts of the world around you.

Then open your eyes. As you gaze all around you, consider the things for which you are thankful. You might consider the following: positive and loving relationships with friends and family, your personal gifts, positive aspects of your health condition, the beauty of your environment, and God's care for you. In whatever way is appropriate give thanks for life's many blessings, recognizing the precious and transitory nature of life itself.

## Questions for Reflection

1) What do think of about the vagueness of Job's identity, ethnicity, or historical context? Is this helpful in your understanding of the text?

2) What do you think about the judgment that Job is "everyman" or "everywoman?"

3) Job regularly performs rituals on behalf of his children, in particular, his sons following their feasts. Using your imagination, what sins might Job's children commit while partying? What do you think about the role of sacrifice to atone for misbehavior?

4) Today, we might call Job a helicopter parent, or co-dependent, in his concern for his children's well-being. In what ways is such parenting helpful? In what ways is it problematic for parent and child?

5) Job's relationship with God appears to be motivated by a combination of gratitude and fear. Reflecting on your own religious life, what role does gratitude play? What role does fear play in relationship to God?

6) How would you describe the relationship of God and ha-satan? Do you think God has agents who note your every deed and report back to God?

7) The first two chapters of Job present a very curious vision of God. What do you think about this initial picture of God? What do you see as the primary characteristics of God, as portrayed in the first section of Job?

8) God withdraws his protection of Job. Do you think God places a protective shield around certain people? Do you think God leaves others at the mercy of circumstance?

9) What do you think is the source of evil in the world? Where does God fit in?

10) How would you evaluate Job's initial responses to losing everything? Would you have responded in the same way? If not, what might be your response to losing everything?

11) How would you describe Job's wife's response? Do you see any insight in her response? What do you think her motivation is for such a strong response to Job's situation?

# A THEOLOGICAL TENNIS MATCH

*In preparation, read Job 2:11-37:34. I will also list shorter readings at the beginning of each section heading.*

Whether the book of Job reflects the work of one or many authors, the brilliance of the final edition of Job is in its blend of poetry and prose and the willingness to address without denial the reality of human suffering and the quest to experience God in the midst of our pain. As I stated earlier, Job leaves us with as many questions as answers. A precursor to postmodernism, Job is content to present many voices and not one orthodox position. God's answer from the whirlwind and the restoration of Job's fortunes continue rather than end the journey of faith. A living faith embraces doubt as well as certainty and questions as well as answers. The text of Job 3:1-42:6 displays an artistic as well as theological genius, inspiring us to deepen our faith and continue our own theological, pastoral, and spiritual adventures.

The theological adventure begins with a brief interlude as Job's friends come on the scene, first with silence and then with solutions.

## A Virtue in Silence

*In preparation, read Job 2:11-13*

Enter Job's friends. They come to comfort and console. No doubt their trips, like some of our own cross country journeys, are arduous and represent sacrifices of time and treasure. They have laid everything aside to support their friend. Their homelands cannot be accurately identified by twenty-first century cartographers. This vagueness suggests that they are also "everyman" and "everywoman," who seeks to comfort and ends up doing more harm than good. Initially, Job's destitution shocks them into silence. All they can do is weep, tear their garments, and cover themselves with dust in solidarity with the physical, relational, and economic devastation Job is experiencing. They join Job at the dump for seven days and seven nights, sitting silently beside him, offering their tears and presence as companionship. They appropriately keep their peace until Job begins the dialogue.

In early 2014, my mother in law, Maxine, passed away at 96 after a good long life. She had lived with us sixteen years and was the ideal, supportive mother-in-law. In the last six months of her life, she began to decline, initially gradually and then rapidly, losing both physical and mental acuity. Intellectual conversations no longer were helpful or necessary. Maxine's caregivers and family simply sat beside her, keeping company and providing care, especially in her last few days. Words were unnecessary. Presence and love were enough as her pilgrimage took her from this lifetime to God's eternal realm.

Job's friends, no doubt, sought to comfort Job by their presence. They had no words to describe the devastation they observed and their own sense of helplessness. They simply sat in vigil, dropping everything to be with him. While pastoral care may involve theological conversations and spiritual counsel, it begins with companionship. Formulas don't work for those who suffer. Even the "right answers" can objectify those who suffer, if they are given without regard to the suffering people are currently experiencing.

Healing initially comes with empathy and listening, embracing the pain of others, before considering any type of physical, emotional, or spiritual remedy.

## The Impatience of Job

### *In preparation, please read Job 3:1-26*

Holistic theology emerges in the interplay of celebration and tragedy. We often forget God's presence in times of joy, thinking that many of our blessings are the result of our own efforts. In contrast, pain focuses our mind on God's role in the suffering we experience. In his classic treatment of the problem of evil, C.S. Lewis asserts, "Pain insists upon being attended to. God whispers to us in our pleasures, speaks in our consciences, but shouts in our pains. It is his megaphone to rouse a deaf world." While I do not agree with Lewis' assumption that God uses pain to wake us up to God's presence, I do believe that pain makes theologians of us all. God works within the pain we feel to awaken us to new behaviors, greater compassion, and alternative priorities.

If you sit on in a garbage dump long enough, you'll lose your cool. Perhaps, Job initially sees his pain as temporary. His equanimity may be as much the result of shock as theological correctness and religious piety. After all, in just the blink of the eye, he loses everything. Initially, Job's pious acceptance might have reflected emotional shutdown rather than unquestioning acceptance of God's ways. After a week at the dump, the harsh reality of his situation may have sunk in. This pain could go on forever. His grief, physical pain, and economic destitution might become the new normal. So, Job lashes out at God, but not as an atheist. His anger comes from his desire to be in relationship with God, and not self-centered pride or denial of God's existence. He wants God to respond, to give him a reason for his pain, and acknowledge his suffering.

Job begins by challenging the fabric of the universe that led to his current state of affairs. Job cries out, "Let the day perish in which I was born, and the night that said, 'Let a man-child be conceived.' Let that day be darkness! May God above not seek it, or light shine on it" (3:3-4)! He continues his tirade against the order of the universe: "Let those curse it who curse the Sea, those who are skilled to rouse up the Leviathan. Let the stars of its dawn be dark...because it did not shut the doors of my mother's womb" (3:8-10, sections).

I live near the ocean and rejoice in my morning walks on Cape Cod's Craigville Beach. I delight in seeing the whitecaps of Nantucket Sound. To the Israelites, however, the sea and the leviathan represent the chaotic elements of the universe. Genesis 1:1-10 describes God's bringing order to a formless void and separating land and sea, giving each its proper domain. In the intricate interdependence of the universe, Job's demand to eliminate the day of his birth would reverse the flow of time and throw everything into chaos.

Job doesn't denounce God, but rues the day he was born. Listen to Job's litany of despair. These are not the calm meditations of a patient man.

> *Why did I not die at birth, come forth from the wound and expire? What were there knees to receive me, or breasts for me to suck? Or why was I not born like a stillborn child...* (3:11-12, 16a)

Job is filled with dread. Although he doesn't curse God, he curses life itself, most particularly the life he is condemned to endure.

> *For my sighing comes like my bread, and my groanings are poured out like water. Truly the thing I fear comes upon me, and what I dread befalls me. I am not at ease, nor am I quiet; I have no rest; but trouble comes.* (3:25-26)

## Let the Games Begin

*In preparation, read Job 4:1-14:23*

When Job's initial acceptance of his condition turns to unbridled anger, his emotional outburst shocks and scandalizes his friends. Job's friends' response changes from empathy to accusation. They want to be helpful, but Job's current state challenges their own understanding of the universe. Like Job, they were successful businessmen, who could afford to make a long journey to see and to support a friend. Like Job, they took their faith seriously and saw a relationship between their personal success and God's blessing. They may have seen their comfortable life as the appropriate reward for personal piety and moral integrity. If Job, whom everyone considers righteous, can be plunged into poverty and pain, there are no guarantees that their stable world might not collapse at any moment. Beginning with Eliphaz, Job's friends seek to explain his current situation, provide a remedy, and bolster their own sense of security.

Their attempts are well-attended but also self-serving. They believe that if Job mends his ways, the rightful order of the universe will be restored. Job will once again be healthy and receive appropriate compensation from God. Job's recovery will assure them of continuing success in their personal and economic life. But Job protests that he is innocent and that God is to blame for his condition. Job's protest continues throughout most of the remainder of the text, threatening the sense of order and security provided by "the old time religion" that all of them, including Job, once affirmed. If goodness is not rewarded, then what can we count on? If there is no connection between righteousness and success, our good works are of no account and the social and religious order will eventually collapse.

It is easy to critique Job's friends. But many of us hold implicitly similar viewpoints. Listen to the speeches of every USA president or of dignitaries at every high school and college graduation and you will a variation on the following: if you get an education, work hard, be a responsible citizen, and obey the law, you can have a share of the American Dream. Think about the words of many preachers who tell us that God favors the righteous and turns away from sinners. Consider all the self-help books that provide easy-to-learn pathways to prosperity, success, and happiness, or promise healthy relationships and stress free parenting. Our society and daily lives depend on the interplay of acts and consequences and rewards and punishments. We tell our children that if they study hard, they will get good grades. Practice is connected with excellence in athletics, art, music, and public speaking. A purely random cosmic and social order in which causes are not connected with effects would lead to personal, relational, and economic chaos. A good life depends on sufficient order and this is most obvious when it comes to issues of health, relationships, education, and economics. A good life also depends on a degree of novelty and unexpectedness, indeed, creative chaos, and that may be one of the lessons of the book of Job.

Job's crisis challenges the easy assumption that following the rules of our faith and society leads to prosperity. It suggests that despite our best efforts to be good spouses, loving parents, hard workers, responsible citizens, and faithful believers, there are no absolute guarantees in life. Contrary to Einstein, God or the universe appears to play dice, and random events can turn our lives upside down. A forty year old, committed to a healthy lifestyle, good eating habits, and regular exercise, dies without warning of a heart attack. A non-smoker, who avoids second hand smoke, is diagnosed with lung cancer. An obese, chain-smoking, alcoholic, curmudgeon, lives to ninety years old and dies quietly in his bed. A dishonest business person, whose business practices bankrupt a company and rob thousands of persons of their life savings, escapes the long arm of justice by fleeing to a country with no extradition treaties.

We can challenge the good fortune of reprobates and assure the faithful of a heavenly reward in the afterlife. We may hope that terrorists, dead beat parents, dishonest business people, and intentional polluters will get what they deserve at the bar of divine justice. But this is not a hope for Job and his friends. They make no reference to post-mortem rewards or punishments. The idea of a positive survival after death had not yet emerged in Hebraic spirituality. Accordingly, they don't look forward to heaven or fear hell. Rewards and punishments must occur in this lifetime for moral and cosmic order to make sense. Sheol, the fate of all mortals, is a shadowy existence, inferior to this-worldly embodied life.

Enter Eliphaz to speak for God's orderly universe and invite Job to mend his ways as the prelude to his personal and economic restoration. Eliphaz's counsel has a certain gravitas. He is not only the oldest of the group; he also claims to have revealed knowledge, arising from a mystical experience. He feels confident, as some do today, to share his admonitions with the prelude, "God told me that …" or "God says …" He trusts his experience of God's wisdom as authoritative and believes it trumps Job's experience of physical and emotional pain and divine abandonment. Listen to Eliphaz's description of his mystical experience:

> *Now a word came stealing to me, my ear received the whisper of it.*
> *Amid thoughts from visions of the night, when deep sleep falls on mortals,*
> *Dread came upon me and trembling which made all my bones shake.*
> *A spirit glided past my face; the hair of my flesh bristled.*
> *It stood still, but I could not discern its appearance.*
> *A form was before my eyes; there was silence, then I heard a voice:*
> *Can mortals be righteous before God? Can human beings be pure before their maker?* (4:12-17)

Eliphaz learns that no creature measures up to God's righteousness. All are suspect and undeserving of divine consideration. On this basis, Eliphaz is certain of Job's guilt. He believes that Job's current situation is the result of his previous sin. The chickens have come home to roost: Job is only reaping what he previously has sown. "Think now, who that was innocent ever perished? As I

have seen, those who plow iniquity and sow trouble reap the same"
(4:7-8),

Whether we speak of divine retribution, the law of compensation, or the workings of karma, the acts-consequences approach
held by Job's friends sees the order of the universe as inexorable.
Punishment awaits evil doers; reward is in store for the righteous.
Job's suffering and loss of economic and social standing testifies to
Job's iniquity. While Eliphaz does not assert an exact correspon-
dence between acts and consequences, it is clear that he believes,
on the basis of divine revelation, that Job is only getting what he
deserves. Over and over throughout the text, Job will hear variations on this theme. Over and over, Job will protest his innocence,
echoing God's own evaluation of his character.

Eliphaz reminds Job that once upon a time he gave such advice
to others and told others that their sufferings were temporary. If
Job gets back on track and mends his ways, this will be a minor
setback in a successful life.

## God, Why Are You Doing This to Me?

*In preparation, read Job 7:1-21; 9:1-10:22*

As the dialogue unfolds, Job expresses his frustration at his
friends. Indeed, with friends like these, who needs enemies, Job
laments! But more devastating, Job experiences what he believes
to be not only the silence of God, but also the malevolence of
God. Job's protests are directed as much to the silent God as to his
talkative friends.

Job believes that directly or indirectly, God is responsible for
the unfolding of the universe. God's providence is displayed in
life's blessings and for most of his life, God's light shined on Job,
giving him health, wealth, and family life. Now, for no apparent
reason, Job has become the object of divine wrath. According to his
understanding of the ways of God with humankind, Job does not
deserve the pain and grief he is experiencing. Like the messages of
today's prosperity gospel preachers or New Age sages, who assert

that faith and righteousness, and positive thinking and spiritual growth, are always reflected in external blessings, Job assumed that his own personal righteousness would lead to continued well-being for himself and his family. If his righteousness is not rewarded, then God's moral nature is compromised and the spiritual edifice upon which he has built his life becomes a sham.

Job sees himself as the target of God's wrath. God has singled him out for undeserved punishment. All pain is personal, even if millions share your same health or economic woes. Listen to Job's complaint. Job's protest has been repeated in hospital rooms, accident scenes, and gravesides.

> *The arrows of the Almighty are in me; my spirit drinks their poison; the terrors of God are arrayed against me.* (6:4)
> *But the night is long, and I am full of tossing until dawn. My flesh is clothed with worms and dirt; my skin hardens, then breaks out again. My days are swifter than a weaver's shuttle, and come to their end without hope.* (7:4-6)
>
> *When I say, "My bed will comfort me, my couch will ease my complaint," then you scare me with dreams and terrify me with visions, so that I would choose strangling and death rather than this body. I loathe my life; I would not live forever. Let me alone, for my days are a breath.* (7:13-16)

Job believes himself to be besieged by a cosmic terrorist who has fixed his sights on him alone, overlooking the faults of the unrighteous. The God whose favor he sought through sacrifice and ethical behavior has intentionally chosen to harm him.

> *For [God] crushes me with a tempest and multiplies my wounds without cause; he will not let me get my breath, but fills me with bitterness.* (9:17)

A fellow human can be evaded or defeated. With God, you cannot run or hide. When the hound of heaven is in pursuit, there is no escape. You must simply suffer, not knowing why or when the suffering will end. Job pleads for mercy from the tormenting

God. He does not expect restoration. His hope and prayer is for the bold lion who hunts him (10:16) to leave him alone so that he might find a little comfort before he sinks into the land of "gloom and deep darkness where light is like darkness" (10:20-21).

## The Silence of God

*In preparation, read Job 15:1-27:23*

Job's God is omnipresent in torment, but absent in communication with his suffering servant. Many of us have felt the same absence of God in times of distress. Pastor and Bible scholar Renita Weems introduces her experiences of divine absence with the words of author Madeleine L'Engle:

> I have often been told that when one turns to God, one is greeted with brilliant Yes answers to prayers. For a long time that was true for me. But, then when [God] has you hooked, he starts to say No. This has been, indeed, my experience. But it has been more than a no answer lately; after all, No is an answer, It is the silence, the withdrawal that is so devastating. The world is difficult enough with God; without him it is a hideous joke.[1]

Renita Weems shares her own experience as a pastor and lecturer of living with God's silence. Though God appeared to have abandoned her in what Weems describes as a season of "spiritual breakdown," she continued her work as a lecturer and pastor. She kept on believing and waiting for God's return, despite her pilgrimage through a divine wasteland. According to Weems:

> Even though I couldn't recall the last time I'd felt anything resembling religious awe or ecstasy, I never stopped praying. I could have walked away from the ordained ministry, of course, and retreated to the lofty heights of academia.... But I decided against that. I chose to remain a minister

---

1   Quoted in Renita Weems, *Listening for God: A Minister's Journey through Silence and Doubt* (New York: Simon and Schuster, 1999), 11.

and to remain actively involved in a congregation, leading worship, administering the sacraments, and leading
prayers. It dawned on me that ministry was precisely
where I needed to be because I no longer recognized the
presence of God in my life. I continued to be a minister
– and I railed against God. Every Sunday, I donned my
clergy stole, prayed for the sick, blessed the sacraments…
spoke about faith, and then came home to sit and stare in
the darkness of my study.[1]

This was Job's experience as well. God is present as the subject
of every protest Jobmakes. God's dynamic power confronts Job in
his distress. God is so present as the source of Job's pain that he
appears to be absent in Job's experience. He calls out to God, and
even enters into a lawsuit compelling God to speak, despite the
divine silence. Twenty-five hundred years later, C.S. Lewis made
the same protest following the death of his wife.

> Of course it's easy enough to say that God seems absent
> at our greatest need because He is absent – non-existent. But,
> then why does He seem so present when, to put it quite frankly,
> we don't ask for him.[2]

Job's life is utterly God-centered. God is as near as his breathing. His "helicopter parent" care that his children be absolved of any
unintended sin reflects his sense of divine concern for the smallest
details of life. God's justice embraces his children's partying as well
as his own commitment to civil duty and care for the indigent.
Nothing gets past God and God is the energy that brings weal and
woe, reward and punishment, in response to human behavior. Job
knows that his "avenger" (often translated "redeemer") lives, but
when will God come out of the shadows to reveal Godself and respond to Job's complaints? Job cries out for theological answers and
relational mercy. He wants restoration and healing, but he receives

---

1   Ibid., 15-16.

2   C.S. Lewis, *A Grief Observed* (New York: Bantam, 1961), 6.

nothing but silence from the ever-compassing, over-functioning, tormenting God he imagines.

Later, we will explore alternatives to Job's initial vision of God. But in meantime, we must see Job's experience in its historical and literary context: Job is righteous, Job is suffering, God is almighty, and this life is all there is in terms of reward and punishment.

Job desires relief and a relationship that can only come from an answering God. "Only grant two things to me, then I will not hide myself from your face; withdraw your hand from me, and do not let dread of you terrify me. Then call, and I will answer; or let me speak, and you reply to me" (13:20-22). God knows – "if I sin, you watch me" (10:14) – and yet does not respond except through the vehicle of punishment. God's silence is deafening. Job believes that his salvation is to be found in conversation with God. If only God will speak, Job will receive the answers he needs, and will accept his punishment or find solace in God's healing presence.

## A Remedy for Job

### *In preparation, read Job 5:17-27; 8:1-22;11:13-20*

Job's friends believe that they have a solution to Job's problems. It is the same solution that Job himself employed in insuring the righteousness of his children: to recognize his children's potential sinfulness and make restitution through rituals of absolution and forgiveness (1:5). In contrast to his friends' solution, Job did not require his children to confess their sins; he always acted on their behalf.

His friends see confession as the first step to restoration. Eliphaz's counsel paves the way for Job to recover his old life. He reminds Job that suffering is educational and corrective. If God lets our sins pass without punishment, eventually we will perish spiritually and physically. "How happy is the one whom God reproves; therefore do not despise the discipline of the Almighty. For he wounds, but he binds up; he strikes but his hands heal"(5:17b-18). Accept your punishment, and mend your ways, and all will be well.

Bildad counsels Job to make confession and seek God's mercy: "If you will seek God, and make supplication to the Almighty, surely then he will rouse himself for you and restore you to your rightful place. Though your beginning was small, your latter days will be very great" (8:5-7). Not to be outdone, Zophar also has friendly advice for suffering Job:

> If you direct your heart rightly, you will stretch out your hands toward him. If iniquity is in your hand, put it far away, and do not let wickedness reside in your tents. Surely then you will lift up your face without blemish; you will be secure and will not fear. You will forget your misery; you will remember it as waters that have passed away. And your life will be brighter than the noonday; its darkness will be like the morning. (11:13-17)

Repentance can transform your life. But Job doubts his friend's promises, especially as these promises appear to rest in a faulty premise: their belief in Job's sinfulness as the source of his malady. Moreover, they assume that a change of heart always leads to changed circumstances.

I believe that our attitudes can shape our health and economic success. In an interdependent universe, our emotional and spiritual lives have a role in overall emotional well-being and life-satisfaction, and they can promote healing. Still, their impact is influenced by a variety of other factors, including prior health conditions, environmental factors, relationships with others, diet and economics, and openness to God's presence. Job's current experience suggests to him that you can do all the right things and still experience economic and relational distress.

Healing and recovery are the gifts of gentle providence and not easy, formulaic answers. Once upon a time, I came upon a book on youth spirituality, entitled *Instant Answers for the King's Kids in Training*. The cover prominently displayed what appeared to be a jar of instant coffee. Now, I like coffee, bold and strong, with a little cream and dash of Stevia. In no way does instant coffee compare with the brands I drink: Starbucks, Gevalia, Paul Newman's, Green Mountain, or Peets. In a similar fashion, fast food can never compare with home cooking, and this same comparison applies to spirituality. Simplistic understandings of sin and redemption, faith and prosperity, or recovery without effort lead to superficial approaches to opening to God's gentle healing touch and letting God heal our cells as well as our souls. Job's healing and recovery won't come from a formula but an open-hearted acceptance of divine providence revealed in the grandeur of life.

## Blaming the Victim

*In preparation, read Job 8:10; 22:1-20; 29:1-31*

Throughout the dialogues of Job and his companions, Job protests his innocence and his friends vehemently maintain his sinfulness. What begins as gentle theology from Eliphaz escalates to character assassination. As I said earlier, Job's friends have some skin in the game. If the orderly universe, supported by the theology they live by is suspect, then their sense of security collapses. If our experiences of good and evil, and joy and pain, have an element of randomness, then we could estimate, no one is safe from the accidents of life. If the evil ones aren't punished and the good aren't rewarded, then why be good? Job's friends are good people, but in a universe that joins providence and chance, and order and chaos, there is no absolute guarantee that goodness will insure a long, healthy, and prosperous life, and that is frightening. They worry that they could end up in the garbage dump, too. Moreover, as their emotions escalate, Job's friends would rather be right than comforting. They neglect Job's suffering, attempting to make Job's experience conform to their theology rather than seeking a holistic vision that joins theology with experience. Job becomes an object to be brow-beaten into submission, all of course, for a good cause, his recovery. Job is no longer a person whose pain evokes empathy, understanding, and care.

Job's friends all hold some variation of Bildad's theological affirmation: "Does God pervert justice? Does the almighty pervert the right?" In the abstract, we can invoke theological platitudes such as "the light of the wicked is put out, and the flame of their fire does not shine" (18:6) or "the wicked writhe in pain all their days" (15:20). But what happens when we personalize our theological abstractions, connecting them to flesh and blood suffering people, dying of cancer, homeless in the wake of a tsunami, or orphaned due to a car accident? Then theology becomes an instrument of torture by which our blaming the victim increases the pain he or she already feels.

Perhaps the cruelest cut of all comes from the lips of Bildad: "If your children sinned against God, God delivered them into the power of their transgression" (Job 8:4). Can you imagine addressing these words to a grieving parent? Sadly, I have heard stories of pastors, claiming inside knowledge of the scales of divine judgment which they felt gave them license to speak of a cause and effect relationship between a parent's sin and a child's cancer, or affirming without a doubt the eternal damnation awaiting an adult child who took his life as a result of depression. Job is no doubt already feeling tremendous guilt, wondering if somehow he forgot to make the appropriate offering to atone for his children's misbehavior. Now he is being told that his children's sin – unconfessed and possibly even unintentional or modest in nature – led to their violent deaths. Job is justified in angrily describing his friends as "quacks" who "white wash with lies." They are "worthless physicians," guilty of theological malpractice by their certainty about divine retribution.

Not to be outdone by his companions' accusatory speeches, the once irenic and mystical Elipaz insults Job's character, judging his former friend and business partner with whom he once spent many a pleasant hour socializing, as an unmitigated reprobate. "Is not your wickedness great? There is no end to your iniquities. You have given no water to the weary to drink, and you have withheld food from the hungry.... You have sent the widow away empty handed, and the arms of the orphan you have crushed. Therefore snares are around you, and sudden terror overwhelms you" (22:5-10). In the heart of the argument, Eliphaz transforms a long-time friend into a lowlife, crook, and demon! This is not an abstract discussion any longer, but a theological fight to the death, in which

Job's defeat will secure in their minds their friends' good fortune and well-being.

Job has no choice but defend his life. He is an innocent victim of divine wrath or, perhaps even more unsettling to his friends, a universe that reflects both chaos and order. In his dialogue with his friends, Job is placed in a Catch 22. If he submits to his friends' accusations and admits to misdeeds he has not committed, he commits a falsehood and may be subject to divine punishment. Conversely, if he maintains his innocence, his friends will continue to harangue him with threats and falsehoods. Job combats his companions' accusations through what he believes to be an accurate description of his previous life: he was once honored and respected by rich and poor and powerful and powerless alike not only because of his wealth but his kindness to vulnerable persons. When Job was a person of financial means and civil power, "he delivered the poor who cried and the orphan who had no helper. The blessing of the wretched came upon [him], and [he] caused the widow's heart to sing for joy....[He] was eyes to the blind, and feet to the lame. [He] was a father to the needy, and [he] championed the cause of the poor" (29:12-17).

Now, Job is alienated from everyone, including his closest friends. Those who honored and respected him, "now make sport of me, those who are younger than I, whose fathers I would have disdained to set with the dogs of my flock" (30:1). Job's words are harsh, but he has been traumatized by God and brutalized personally and theologically by his friends. If he has committed evil, he is willing to face divine punishment (31:1-5). But Job has never violated the religious, relational, and social mores of his community. Remember, that although Job is unaware of it, he is righteous in God's eyes, the man whose integrity God trusts without question.

## A Random Universe?

*In preparation, read Job 12:1-21; 21:1-34*

Job is looking for justice in the universe. The orthodoxy that once guided his life no longer works. His own mortal flesh has proven it wrong. Goodness is not always rewarded. Evil is not always punished. Once again, remember the subtext:

- Job's long-held theology affirms a linear, closed-system understanding of acts and consequences, insuring that we always get what we deserve in life.
- Job is deemed righteous by God, and can find no fault in himself commensurate with the suffering he and his family have experienced.
- Job's theology is entirely this-worldly. There is no heaven to look forward to or hell to fear. There is no afterlife to balance the scales of justice. Reward and punishment must occur in this lifetime.
- Job's suffering opens his eyes to the reality that life appears unjust: the righteous suffer and the evil prosper.

Job's assertion of randomness in the universe, and in the execution of divine justice, is the last straw for his friends. Job has utterly denied the truth all of them have lived by. He has taken the rug out from under their secure universe. Job's theology moves from the theoretical to the empirical as a result of his pain. He sees the world more clearly from a garbage dump than he did from his luxurious home.

> *The tents of the robbers are at peace, and those who provoke God are secure, who bring their God into their own hands.* (12:6)
> *Why do the wicked live on, reach old age and grow mighty in power? Their children are established in their presence and their offspring before their eyes. Their houses are safe from fear, and no rod of God is upon them.* (21:7-9)
> *How often is the lamp of the wicked put out? How often does calamity come upon them? How often does God distribute*

*pains in his anger?....You say, "God stores up their iniquity for
their children."....One dies in prosperity, being wholly at ease and
secure, his loins full of milk and the marrow of his bones moist.
Another dies in bitterness of soul, never having tasted of good.
They lie down alike in the dust, and the worms cover them.*
(Job 21: 17, 19a, 23-27)

Job is not denying the value of virtue or the importance of
worship. Job still affirms the existence of God. But he is questioning the moral order of the universe: Do we reap what we sow in
exact measure? Is there free play in the outcome of our actions?
Does God play by our rules, giving us what we deserve or is there
an inherent amorality in God's majesty? Does the universe and the
unfolding of our lives exhibit chance as well as order? Can we do
all the right things in our parenting, economic lives, marriages,
religious practice, and civic duty and still fail to experience happiness and personal fulfilment? Is divine justice ultimately blind,
arbitrary and uncaring?

Job's observations are those of a believer. His quest for righteousness compels him to look at life as it is, noting the tragic
nature of life and not denying suffering through orthodox theological reflection.

## A Passionate Young Man

*In preparation, read Job 32:6-37:24*

When I served as university chaplain, I often encountered
passionate young Christians. Though just first year college students,
they were on fire for God and often shared their faith with little or
no consideration for the feelings of those they addressed. From the
perspective of their black and white religious and ethical systems,
they were clear about objective truth and about others' falsehood.
They often judged others' behaviors or belief systems without getting to know either the person or the context. In the spirit of a
former USA president, they did not do nuance!

Enter Elihu, a young man who enters the dialogue out of no-where, leading some scholars to believe his character is the result of a later addition to the text. Elihu is passionate, orthodox, and absolutely certain of his position. Sitting on the sidelines, observing the theological tennis match between Job and his friends, Elihu is seething. Job's heretical suggestions make his blood boil and the theological and rhetorical ineptness of Job's friends, with whom he basically agrees, is even more distressing. Elihu's state of mind and intent are summarized by the following words:

> *Elihu, son of Barachel, the Buzite, of the family of Ram, became angry. He was angry at Job because he justified himself rather than God; he was angry also at Job's friends because they had found no answer, though they had declared Job to be in the wrong.* (32:2-3)

Elihu begins by confessing his initial reticence. He yields to the wisdom of the elders, but discovers age does not necessarily bring understanding or wisdom. Despite his youth, he is taking center stage and he will set everyone straight. He must declare the truth or remain silent in denial of his faith. "My heart is like wine that has no vent; like new wineskins it is ready to burst. I must speak so that I may find relief; I must open my lips and answer" (32:19-20).

Despite his sense that his words inject truth and novelty into the dialogue, Elihu's theology closely resembles that of Job's friends. First, he challenges Job's assertion that God is silent. Elihu correct-ly, in my mind, affirms that God's guidance comes in many ways, including dreams and visions, whose purpose is to alert us to our errors and set us on the right path (33:13-18). In addition, how-ever, Elihu believes that God also chastens humanity with pain, whose severity leads first to confession and then salvation (33:19-28). Moreover, Elihu affirms the justice and righteousness of God. "According to their deeds, God will repay them, and according to their ways he will make it befall them....God will not pervert justice" (34:10-12). God knows all and will strike evil doers for their wickedness (34:21-30). Elihu believes that Job is in for more trouble. His questioning of God's ways will lead to further punishment. God's ways are without reproach; our doubts and questions are a sign of infidelity and an invitation to rebuke.

> *Would that Job were tried to the limit, because his answers are those of the wicked. For he adds rebellion to his sin; he claps his hands among us, and multiplies his words against God.* (34:36-37)

Elihu concludes with words that appear to be a prelude to God's speech from the whirlwind. Elihu rejoices in God's righteousness and justice, and invites Job and his friends to consider the majesty of God. Elihu could easily have penned the words of the hymn, *How Great Thou Art*, so great is his awe at God's creativity and might (37:1-24).

Elihu's heart is in the right place. In his estimation, God is everything and we are nothing. He must speak for God's honor and rebuke Job for his doubt of God's goodness and justice. It is unclear, however, that Elihu is any more successful in persuading Job of his sin than Job's friends. Job becomes speechless not as a result of Elihu's passionate defense of divine justice, but in response to the sound of God's own voice. Theologically correct, Elihu is personally and pastorally inept. His bombast is like that of a street corner preacher, who proclaims God's coming wrath, but never looks into the eyes of those who pass him by. The mere fact that they fail to respond immediately to his diatribe is a sign of their waywardness and eventual doom. Yet, a preacher without love soon becomes a "noisy gong or a clanging cymbal" (1 Corinthinas 13:1)

## Journeying with Job

As a spiritual practice, take time today to practice silence. Observe any tendencies to correct others' theological or ideological mistakes. When you feel compelled to set them straight, pause and notice your need to be right. What spiritual or emotional issue compels you to notice others' errors in contrast to your rightness? Take time throughout the day to pray for the ability to understand others' actions and life situations.

Silence is not an agreement or failure to challenge injustice or harmful behaviors. It is an opportunity to truly listen to and ask for God's guidance in your interpersonal relationships.

Take several opportunities throughout the day to pause and take note of God's presence in your life and in those with whom you interact.

## Questions for Reflection

1) In what ways is entertaining many theological voices helpful to a growing spiritually? In what ways might a pluralism of faith possibilities be problematic?

2) How do you respond to the pain of others? In what ways are you like Job's friends? In what might your response differ from them?

3) How you have responded initially to traumatic events affecting you as well as others? What was most helpful to you in gaining some perspective on the trauma you experienced or observed?

4) Job finally lashes out at God. In what ways is anger at God helpful? In what ways might anger at God be ambiguous or problematic spiritually?

5) Job's friends' criticism of his beliefs may reflect their own anxiety about the precariousness of their own situation. Have you experienced theology being used to bolster peoples' economic or social well-being and sense of entitlement?

6) According to Job's friends, why is Job in such a mess? What remedy do they suggest to restore him to his former life situation?

7) What difference do religious rituals make in our lives? Do you think they can transform our personal and economic lives?

8) In what ways does social order and family life depend on the acts-consequences, reward-punishment approach to life? Is this always bad? Does a sense of consequences serve a positive social and interpersonal function? When does

an acts-consequences approach become theologically and personally problematic?

9) What do you think of Eliphaz's mystical experience? Have you ever had a self-transcendent or mystical experience?

10) How would you describe Job's spiritual and theological crisis? Is his sense of injustice warranted?

11) What do you think of calling God a "cosmic terrorist?" Have you ever felt picked out by God for good or bad fortune?

12) What do you think of Renita Weems' decision to remain active in ministry despite her pervasive experience of God's absence? What would you do in her shoes?

13) How would you respond to Job's friends' remedy to his suffering? Does ritual and repentance always change our life for the good?

14) Consider the following remedies. Do you think they are helpful?

> *How happy is the one whom God reproves; therefore do not despise the discipline of the Almighty. For he wounds, but he binds up; he strikes but his hands heal. (5:17b-18)*

> *If you direct your heart rightly, you will stretch out your hands toward him. If iniquity is in your hand, put it far away, and do not let wickedness reside in your tents. Surely then you will lift up your face without blemish; you will be secure and will not fear. You will forget your misery; you will remember it as waters that have passed away. And your life will be brighter than the noonday; its darkness will be like the morning. (11:13-17)*

15) How would you respond to Bildad's comments about Job's children in some way deserving their deaths? Have you heard religious leaders identifying personal suffering with sin?

 # WISDOM FROM THE WHIRLWIND

*In preparation, read Job 28:1-28; 38:1-41:34*

Out of nowhere, the voice of God emerges from a whirlwind. The text suggests that God is directly responding to Job, and that the original dialogue ends at Job 31:30, "the words of Job are ended," with Elihu's words as a latter addition. Job hears but never sees God:

> *Then the Lord answered Job out of the whirlwind:*
> *"Who is this that darkens counsel by words without knowledge?*
>
> *Gird up your loins like a man, I will question you, and you shall declare to me." (38:1-3)*

The deafening silence of God gives way to an equally deafening storm. There is no still small voice in this passage, but the voice of thunder and tornado, infinite and untamed. Be careful what you pray for! Job hopes for a gentle presence and a rational explanation from the Holy One. He receives a vision of divine majesty and creativity, the power and energy that brought forth the universe from a speck smaller than a fingertip.

God becomes the inquisitor now, and Job the respondent. God doesn't ever answer Job's questions, justify his actions, or give a reason for Job's suffering. This isn't divine bullying but a peek into the inner workings of our majestic, marvelous, and sometimes risky universe. God shows Job the panorama of the universe in its grandeur. In line with Hebraic theology, God never reveals his own grandeur directly to Job; Job is overwhelmed by the wonders springing from divine creativity, going beyond anything mortals can imagine. Listen to a selection of God's questions:

> *Where were you when I laid the foundation of the earth?* (38:4)
>
> *Who laid the earth's cornerstone's when the morning stars sang together and all the heavenly beings shouted for joy?* (38:6a-7)
>
> *Who shut the in the sea with doors when it burst out from the womb?.... Thus far you shall you come, and no farther, and here your proud waves be stopped?* (38:8,11)

As a resident of a seaside community on Cape Cod, I am always amazed that even on a stormy day, with white caps on the Nantucket Sound, there is a limit to the ocean's power. I can imagine the awe the Israelites, whose comfort zone was limited to the Sea of Galilee, experienced when they considered God's restraint of the wind and the waves.

God's dialogue moves from earth to heaven, inviting Job to consider the cosmos in all its grandeur.

> *Can you bind the chains of the Pleiades or loose the cords of Orion?*
>
> *Can you lead forth the Mazzaroth in their season, or can you guide the Bear with its children? Do you know the ordinances of the heavens? Can you establish their rule on the earth?* (38:31-33)

The author of Psalm 8 experienced this same awe as he reflected on the infinity of God and the finitude of humankind:

> *O Lord, our Sovereign,*
> *How majestic is your name in all the earth!*
> *You have set your glory about the heavens....*
> *When I look at your heaven, the work of your fingers,*
> *the moon and stars that you have established;*
> *what are human beings that you are mindful of them,*
> *mortals that you care for them?* (Psalm 8:1, 3-4)

Job beholds God's handiwork that brings order to chaos and provides the dependable environment necessary for human flourishing. The pain and suffering we experience is grounded in an orderly and mostly predictable universe. Without the requisite order, we could not exist nor could we experience the dissonance created by the contrast of sickness with health.

Chapters 39-41 could be titled, in the spirit of Maurice Sendak's book, "where the wild things are." God's tour of the universe moves back to earth with descriptions of wild goats, donkeys, and oxen, and then the foolishness of the ostrich. All creation, in its wonder and wildness, reflects divine creativity. The universe is orderly and dependable, but also playful and chaotic. We may be able to tame oxen and donkeys for a season, but it is in their nature to defy human-made order. Horses can be harnessed but they also can bolt or rear up, putting our lives at risk.

The divine tour of the universe now highlights two mythical creatures, behemoth and leviathan. Though often identified with the hippopotamus and crocodile, respectively, my own approach is to see leviathan and behemoth as symbolic of the chaotic and untamed elements of the universe. God creates and restrains these mythical creatures, but they have a wildness and unpredictability with which even God must contend. There are always pockets of chaos in the world and in our lives, from the cellular to the spiritual level.

The voice of the whirlwind ends as abruptly as it begins. God's final words are a hymn to leviathan, "On earth it has no equal, a creature without fear. It surveys everything that is lofty; it is king over all that are proud" (41:33-34).

Job's response is a confession of his finitude in comparison to God's grandeur. "Therefore I have uttered what I did not understand, things too wonderful for me which I did not know...I had heard of you by the hearing of my ear; but now my eyes see you; therefore I despise myself, and repent in dust and ashes" (42:3b, 5-6). Dwarfed by God's majesty, all Job can do is acknowledge his limitations of power and knowledge. He still cannot fathom "the problem of evil" or the causes of his own suffering. But his mystical experience gives him a new perspective on life, within which even his suffering has a place. The tapestry of divine creativity includes creation and destruction, and life and death. Job's pain is real, but it is relativized in light of his new understanding of the world, as the result of divine intentionality and creaturely randomness, divine purpose and mortal chaos.

## Where Shall Wisdom Be Found?

The theological interlude found in Chapter 28 provides a lens through which to view Job's mystical experience. The unknown speaker of Chapter 28 – could it be God? – asks "Where shall wisdom be found? Where does wisdom come from? And where is the place of understanding" (28:12,20)? Hidden from human pride and beyond everyday experience, wisdom emerges from the "fear of the Lord" (28:28). Encountering God may leave us with fear and trembling. A universe of more than 125 billion galaxies overwhelms us and reduces us to silence, and the intricacy of the human body inspires amazement. However, the fear associated with wisdom is really a form of awe at the wonder of the universe and infinite power of the creativity which brings forth life in all its myriad forms.

Job's awe at encountering God does not answer his questions. It gives him something more. It awakens him to his place as God's companion in a wild and wonderful universe.

## Journeying with Job

Job's life is transformed by a mystical experience of God's grandeur and the wonders of the universe. Rabbi Abraham Joshua Heschel once asserted that "radical amazement" is at the heart of the religious experience. Take time today to simply consider the wonders of the universe. Perhaps, you can view a segment of Neil deGrasse Tyson's *Cosmos*, gaze upon photos from the Hubble Telescope, or better yet awaken with the sunrise and gaze at the night sky. Take time read the words of Psalms 8 and 148-150 and meditate on their vision of the universe. Explore the possibility of practicing to experience "God in all things and all things in God."

## Questions for Reflection

1) One commentator describes God as a cosmic bully trying to intimidate Job by divine power. How do you respond to this evaluation of the voice from the whirlwind?

2) If you were to perceive the universe as God displays it to Job, how would you respond?

3) What are your feelings when you consider the grandeur of the universe and the finitude of humankind?

4) In what ways does Job's vision of the universe serve as the source of a new perspective on life? If you were in his shoes, how would your sense of your suffering change, if at all?

5) How do we balance the importance of our lives and what we do on our planet with our minor placement in the universe?

6) What you think of the notion that order is necessary for us to experience chaos?

7) Why do you think God chooses the ostrich as an example of divine handiwork? What lessons can we learn from this interesting creature?

8) In what ways is the introduction of behemoth and leviathan examples of divine artistry? In what ways do they reveal order? In what ways might they be symbols of chaos?

9) What is the source of Job's repentance? How does this shape his challenge to God's justice? Does Job or God ever admit to Job's unrighteousness?

10) Meditate on Psalm 8. What images of the universe do you see? What images of humankind? Can we be both small and important at the same time?

 # JOB'S RESTORATION

*In preparation, read Job 42:1-17*

"I wish that Job had ended with Job's confession and not his restoration (Job 42:6)," Emily averred. "The ending ties things up in a pretty package and puts a bow on it. Everything's solved and that's not real life, certainly not my life. The ending's too much like a Hallmark movie or happy ever after fairy tale."

Jim added, "I wonder if Job still felt the trauma of losing everything. Did he grieve the loss of his children? Despite his new wealth and replacement children, did he always look over his shoulder, wondering if he would lose everything again or if the God of the universe could be trusted with his little life?"

Beth noted in response to Emily, "I don't know what to think of the replacement children. Did they truly replace the ones Job lost? I know friends who've had children born following miscarriages and deaths. They always remember the child they lost, in spite of their love for their other children."

Jack added, "You never get over the loss of a child, and I don't think Job did either."[1]

Like the participants at my Job Bible studies at South Congregational Church, I also feel a bit uneasy with the concluding verses of Job. I wonder if the final editor wanted to meet orthodoxy in the middle. Perhaps, he felt that the theological tennis match and divine whirlwind had gone too far and might undermine the

---

1 I have changed the names of these Bible study participants to preserve privacy and reflect my own interpretations of their comments.

mores necessary for a civil society. Did he want to assert that the acts-consequences approach to the fate of the righteous and unrighteous had an element of truth to it, despite Job's scathing critique of the theory?

As we read the text, we may ask, "For what is Job being rewarded anyway?" He questioned God's goodness and care. He even wanted to file a lawsuit against the Creator. Job never gave up on his innocence, despite being overwhelmed by the voice in the whirlwind, whose overwhelming display of the universe in its variety never truly responded to Job's deepest questions.

Could it be that Job's reward emerges from God's recognition of the constancy of Job's commitment to dialogue with the Holy One? Job never denied God's existence and presence in his life. He simply could no longer believe in a God who arranges the world in terms of rewards and punishments. His old vision of God died and a new one is in the process of being born. Perhaps, that's the point: Job is right all along in spite of his limitations. God's nature differs from the acts-consequences piety that he affirmed during his days of prosperity. God doesn't conform to our limited visions of good and evil, nor does God favor certain people, the religiously righteous, at the expense of others. The divine majesty, emerging from the whirlwind, reveals God's creative wisdom and energy giving life to all creatures, both predator and prey, moving even through the apparent randomness of life. As Jesus asserted several centuries later, "God makes the sun shine on the evil and the good, and sends rain on the righteous and on the unrighteous" (Matthew 5:45).

Perhaps, Job's faithfulness, despite his doubts and complaints, reveals a deeper faith than the orthodoxy he and his friends affirmed without question. Job's "reward" may be the unexpected gift arising from his faithful agnosticism – his willingness to dialogue with God in all of his challenges and doubts. In the midst of his own personal and theological whirlwind, Job may have discovered the promise given by the Apostle Paul, whether we live or die, we belong to God (Romans 14:8). The reward is not monetary compensation for damages incurred by divine "evil," but the discovery that God is present through all the struggles and storms of life as the power of possibility and beauty in all the seasons of life. There are no guarantees of economic or political reward in our dynamic and risky universe. There is the guarantee that God has "the whole world – including my suffering – in God's hands."

## What Did We Do Wrong?

Emily wondered about the fate of Job's friends. "In their minds they were the proponents of orthodoxy. They were standing up for good and justifying God's ways to Job. They wanted to restore moral order to the universe. You'd think God would reward them. Why does God turn on them? Maybe God isn't as orthodox as we think." Although she was once an adherent of a rewards-punishments vision of heaven and hell, Sharon experienced a theological upheaval as a result of a vivid dream about heaven. "I dreamed that heaven was filled with Buddhists and Hindus, Muslims and new agers. My deceased relatives who left the church in adulthood were there too! Maybe God is different than I thought. Maybe my standards were too narrow and unbending, while God is much more broad-minded and flexible than I was taught as a child."

I am sure that Job's friends were astounded to be on receiving end of divine judgment. The author of Job goes so far as to suggest that the all-too-human God portrayed in the first two chapters is now filled with wrath at their responses to Job's situation. "But how could God be angry at us?" Job's friends must have thought. "After all, we have lived righteous lives and believed all the right things. We were trying to set Job straight, and help him return to an orthodox understanding of God's ways with humankind. What we said was for his own good and to help him regain his faith and fortune? Isn't that what God would want us to do?"

What could their fault have been? Could their error have been pastoral and relational as well as theological? In trying to fit Job's experiences into a neat theological box, they may have unintentionally placed the Creator in an equally tight theological box. Moreover, their theological reflection was harmful rather than healing. When they sat quietly before Job, sharing in his agony, they comforted his spirit. But, the moment they tried to convert him to the old time religion, they forgot his pain. In fact, they used his pain as a theological weapon, connecting the pain he felt and his personal and economic losses with his sinful behavior. To uphold their orthodoxy, they needed an enemy, and Job fit the bill. The only way their theological world view could be salvaged was by savaging Job with the righteousness of their orthodoxy. If Job was right about the randomness of the universe, then their tightly-held orthodoxy would have to be abandoned.

Centuries later, Jesus counseled his followers, "as you have done unto the least of these, my brothers and sisters, you have done unto me" (Matthew 25:40). In blaming the victim Job for his suffering, they added to Job's pain and according to Jesus' affirmation, the pain of God.

The Hippocratic Oath also applies to theological counsel: "First, do no harm." The moment Job's friends moved the focus of their relationship with suffering Job from pastoral care to doctrinal orthodoxy, they had to sacrifice Job at the altar of theological correctness. Their belief system became more important than his anguish.

Theology is important and what we believe and how we share our beliefs can cure or kill, comfort or traumatize. Still, theological correctness pales in importance to responding to human pain. The Voice in the Whirlwind may be oblivious to our theological orthodoxies, but the Creator of a wondrous world of diversity and beauty, mixed with pain and suffering, is concerned with the well-being of suffering creatures. Whoever leads one of these little ones astray or harms a fellow human by placing doctrine ahead of compassionate care incurs God's judgment. And, in light of God's call for a sacrificial offering, such theological hard heartedness puts into question the possibility of God's forgiveness as well!

Job's friends must do what they had urged Job to do: repent of their wrongdoing, make a sacrifice, and restore their relationship with their estranged friend. Job also receives a mission. He must restore his friends' relationship to God – and himself - by praying for their well-being and safety. His forgiveness is part of his own healing process. In forgiving them, he was forgiving his own previous theological malpractice and judgments about others' life circumstances, and the impact of his former beliefs on others. As righteous as Job may have been, his acts-consequences theology built a wall between him and those who are tormented by illness, accident, and poverty. His scrupulous performance of sacrifices on behalf of his children may have reflected his own inability to trust God's ultimate care for the universe in its complexity. In praying for his friends' forgiveness, Job himself receives a spiritual blessing, described in terms of his economic, relational, and family restoration.

Yet there is some irony in his friends' restoration. Job is asked to provide a remedy that he found reprehensible during his time of trial. Is the author of this passage trying to affirm that ritual is important in personal transformation even if he or she has doubts about a linear understanding of ritual and healing? After deviating so far from orthodoxy, is he or she seeking common ground with those whose theologies have been challenged in the text? Perhaps there is some truth in their position, provided it is understood in flexible and pastoral terms.

## Job's Restoration

The book of Job concludes with Job receiving twice as much wealth as he had before, ten new children, and a return to his previous status in the community. Even Job's relatives, who seemed to be absent during his darkest times, return to share their sympathy for all that he has suffered at the hand of God. Despite Job's reversal of fortunes, God's treatment of his righteous follower is described as "evil." No amount of restoration can fully compensate for the pain that Job experienced as a result of the loss of his first family and his personal health and economic status. Job will always be wounded, for he has been touched by tragedy, just as the Risen Christ is recognized by his wounds and not his perfection.

In addition to receiving seven new sons, Job receives three daughters, who are described as the most beautiful women in the land. Further, in a move uncharacteristic of a patriarchal time, the names of Job's daughters are mentioned – Jemimah, Keziah, and Karen-happuch -- while his sons are left unnamed. In a time in which women seldom inherited their father's wealth, the author notes that Job's lovely daughters receive an inheritance along with their brothers. In light of his suffering and destitution, perhaps Job wishes to insure economic security, independent of marriage, for his daughters.

The passage concludes with a description of Job's life as truly abundant. He dies having left a legacy of beauty embodied in four generations of descendants. Psychiatrist Robert Jay Lifton speaks of five types of immortality:

- biological: leaving a legacy of children;
- creative: making a mark on future generations by your actions and creative work;
- natural: feeling a kinship with the larger universe from which our lives emerge;
- experiential transcendence: transformation through mystical experience; and
- theological: survival after death.

Job truly fulfilled his destiny, as understood in his cultural and religious context:

- he left heirs and saw his great grandchildren's births
- he shaped peoples' lives economically and spiritually
- he experienced the wonders of nature and was taken beyond himself to experience the world mystically from God's perspective.

Survival after death is not promised in Job's culture, but he has lived a good life. Ultimately, Job embodies philosopher Alfred North Whitehead's notion of tragic beauty, the creative weaving together of pain, joyful achievement, and meaning for future generations. I suspect Job gave thanks for the blessings of his abundant new life. I also believe that he, like Jesus, wore the scars of grief, life-threatening illness, and personal and economic collapse. Beauty does not exclude pain and struggle but places them in the broader perspective of God's wondrous, yet risky, universe.

## Journeying with Job

In today's spiritual practice, pray with your eyes open. Notice the pain of the world as revealed in the persons you meet in the course of a day, the headlines in the paper or online, or in news programs you watch or listen to. Throughout the day, meditate upon Jesus' affirmation that "as you have done unto the least of these you have done unto me." Where are you called to reach out to the vulnerable? Which persons reveal Christ to you and call you to be Christ-like in your behavior?

## Questions for Reflection

1) What is your response to the comment: "I wish that Job had ended with Job's confession and not his restoration."?

2) Continuing, how would you evaluate the following comment? "I wonder if Job still felt the trauma of losing everything. Did he grieve the loss of his children? Despite his new wealth and replacement children, did he always look over his shoulder, wondering if he would lose everything again or if the God of the universe could be trusted with his little life?" Do you think the story ends too quickly and predictably?

3) Are the righteous always rewarded at the end of the day? Have you ever seen moral people end up in despair and hopelessness, destitute and alone? How do you account for that?

4) As the story ends, for what is Job being rewarded? What ideas come to mind?

5) How might Job's friends have felt when they discovered themselves as the objects of divine wrath? What did they do wrong to incur God's ire? Did they deserve God's wrath?

6) How is the Hippocratic Oath, "first, do no harm," an important theological maxim? Have you seen theology harm people? Have you seen theology be an instrument of healing and grace?

7) What do you think of the irony of Job making sacrifices on behalf of his friends, especially after his doubts about the acts-consequences approach to good and bad fortune?

8) What do you think of Job's restoration? Do think the "replacement" children really replaced the ones who had died? What's the point of this process of restoration?

9) What do you think of Job's good death? For him, death is the end. Can you have a meaningful life without survival after death?

10) What do you think of the emphasis on Job's daughters in this passage? What meaning might it have then and now?

11) As you look at the book of Job, what is the greatest insight you find in the text? In what ways has it changed your perspective?

# THEOLOGY'S MANY VOICES

The Voice from the Whirlwind has spoken and Job's fortunes have been restored. His righteousness has been reaffirmed by the Almighty. Job's silence and humility inspire divine generosity. Job's God, however, remains mysterious and inscrutable. God creates a universe that is orderly and predictable, and yet wild and untamed. God's glory is infinite and God's providence is sovereign over all things. God's love, however, is still in doubt. Does God treasure creation in its parts as well as in the majestic totality? Is God willing to suffer and go to the cross on our behalf? Or, as Carl Jung asserts in his analysis of the Book of Job: Job is moral, but God is amoral. We can feel wonder and awe, and fear such a deity, but can we love a God who rules all things, regardless of its negative impact on creation?

In the final chapters of this book, we move from text to theology, inspired by our empathy with Job's suffering and our own questions about the relationship of God's power and human pain. We will consider questions that the author of Job raised in light of the theological pluralism of twenty five centuries. Old Testament scholar Terence Fretheim believes the most important question of faith is not "Do you believe in God?" but "What is the character of the God in whom we believe?" Is God defined primarily by power or love? Does God care about us enough to empathize and feel our pain? Further, in light of Job's friends' belief that religious rituals provide a remedy to Job's suffering, we will consider the power of prayer in an uncertain universe.

Our theology is both practical and pastoral. How we view the universe and God's role in shaping our lives will determine our response to those who suffer and our understanding of the power of prayer to change our life circumstances. Our journey will begin with a review of what academic and popular everyday theologians have identified as the sources of suffering and pain, as they relate to God and the nature of the universe. The particular themes we will explore have emerged as much from my conversations with laypeople, many of whom have suffered much, as well the insights of the great theologians and philosophers. Accordingly, I have chosen several approaches, mirroring the book of Job's many voices, including that of Job and his friends, as windows for understanding the problem of pain and the apparently unjust distribution of suffering in our world.

## What's the Problem?

The problem of suffering is never abstract even when it's posed by armchair theologians. Eventually everyone who believes in God has to deal with the apparently unfair distribution of suffering in the world. For the past few weeks, my heart has been broken as I pray for the nearly 300 hundred Nigerian girls, kidnapped by an Islamic fundamentalist sect. The members of Boko Haram are sure that God is all powerful, that they know God's will as explicitly stated in the Qur'an, despite the fact most Muslims condemn their violence. Inspired by their vision of a sovereign, inflexible, and merciless god, they believe that they are instruments of divine justice toward the infidel. They are certain God is on their side and that their cause is just despite the suffering it is causing innocent children. In their orderly universe, despite their youthful innocence, the Nigerian girls are only getting what they deserve for following Western ways.

As a pastor, my heart is touched by families dealing with issues of substance abuse and life-threatening cancer, and the pain of adult children and spouses whose loved ones no longer recognize them as a result of Alzheimer's disease. Our weekly congregational intercessory prayers lift up the pain caused by alcoholism, drug addiction, incurable illness, motorcycle accidents, and post-traumatic stress. It is natural that as we pray for God's healing touch, often asking for a miracle or a dramatic burst of God's energy to restore people to wholeness, that we also wonder what role God has in the pain and suffering of our world.

Job experienced pain first hand as his experience of grief, bankruptcy, and illness turned his world upside down. Job believed the following things that made his suffering both a personal and theological issue:

- God is just and has established a dependable order of acts and consequences, insuring that the righteous flourish and the unrighteous suffer.
- God is able to do anything God desires. God is all-powerful, determining the events of our lives.
- Job is righteous and deserves all of life's blessings. He deserves the continuation of the good fortune he has experienced throughout his adult life.
- Job is suffering for no apparent reason, and this suffering must be attributable, in some mysterious way, to God's will.

Job never lets go of his sense of personal righteousness. Nor does he deny God's power.

Divine justice, morality, and care are at stake.

In many ways, Job's experiential theology is a model for all future theodicies, or attempts to make sense of evil and suffering in a God-created world. Traditionally, the philosophical problem of evil is described in the following way:

- God is just and loving.
- A loving and just God would want to eliminate suffering and pain.
- God is all powerful and can shape every possible state of affairs.
- An all-powerful God could eliminate suffering and pain.

- Suffering and pain, much of it apparently unnecessary and arbitrary, exists.
- Accordingly, God is either not all-powerful or all-loving. Which will it be?

For God to be all-powerful, just, and all-loving, the suffering of the world must serve a greater good for those who suffer and for the world as a whole, and according to some theologians, non-human creatures as well. Our sufferings must lead to greater strength in character and compassion, or be resolved in the afterlife, where all eventually are saved. If one is lost, who could be saved, even if this is a result of her or his choice, this represents either a failure of love, power, or justice on God's part.

## Worship His Majesty?

A favorite hymn in many evangelical circles is Jack Hayford's *Worship His Majesty*. I have to admit that that it is a catchy tune with pithy lyrics. While I am sure that Hayford believes God loves humanity, or at least those who are "saved," there is not one word about love in the song. We exalt majesty, authority, power, and being chosen, none of which, in and of themselves, imply compassion, empathy, or love for humankind and the non-human world. The cross of Christ reflects God's love for the world, but, despite Hayford's vision of divine sovereignty, the power of the cross to save is limited by the decisions of mere mortals and God's own demand that divine justice lead to the damnation of unbelievers.

Church of the Nazarene theologian, Thomas Oord, has noted that the Christian theological tradition has often seen power as more important than love in describing God's nature and relationship with the world.[1] If power is the most important divine characteristic, then there is no problem of evil. Whatever God wills is good, regardless of its impact on us, simply because God wills it.

John Calvin is perhaps the boldest exponent of sovereignty and all-determining power as the primary characteristic of God. God is beyond good and evil. God's power is displayed in everything that

1    Thomas Oord, *The Nature of Love: A Theology* (Chalice Press, 2010).

occurs, regardless of its impact on our lives. Not a raindrop falls or leaf stirs without God's expressed will. Every heart beat and cancer cell reflects God's majesty. Before the world was created, God determined every event; all things reflect God's good pleasure. God determines who will be saved, and who will be damned, apart from any decisions on our part. The world is a theatre of God's glory. God owes us nothing, but chooses to save certain members of fallen humankind out of God's sovereign mercy. God's love embraces God's elect; the rest are merely agents of divine wrath. The elect are blessed with the signs of grace and election, while the lost – rightly described as the reprobate – may appear to prosper but will eventually experience well-deserved eternal damnation as sinners in the hands of an angry God. The lost have no rights and cannot alter the godforsaken future. They are surely damned if they do, and damned if they don't.

Our pain and suffering ultimately do not matter in Calvin's universe. If we perceive ourselves to be among God's elect, we must accept the good and evil as the working out of God's plan for us and live with the hope that divine providence has destined us for life everlasting in the communion of saints. It's not about us at all; it's all about God's all-determining will being enacted in our lives. The death of a young parent from heart disease or a child from cancer is merely the working out of God's all-determining power. Our pain is ultimately of no consequence to the Almighty!

Job and his friends initially believe that God's power is unlimited. Throughout the text, Job and his friends assume that all things reflect God's power. Evil and good alike come to humankind as a result of divine activity. Later, however, Job expects a dialogical relationship with God in which God must justify his apparently unfair treatment of God's faithful and righteous servant. Job begins to question a vision of God which suggests that divine power is amoral and unconcerned with its impact on humankind.

Images of divine sovereignty are alive and well in the twenty first century. In fact, I have found that many people are more reticent to question God's omnipotence, his unrestricted ability to achieve his will, than God's love. They can live with God causing cancer or a devastating earthquake, but worry that a loving God might not be powerful enough to insure that God's will be done in defeating his enemies, including Satan at the end of history. Of course, God's moral will and care for humanity seem to be defied on a regular basis by the incidence of incurable cancer, child abuse, sex trafficking, natural catastrophe, and political violence.

Rick Warren's best-selling *Purpose Driven Life* represents a hybrid theological vision: Warren affirms a form of divine predestination, yet leaves room for human freedom in responding to God's all-determining will. According to Warren,

> God's purpose for your life predates your conception. He planned it before you existed, without your input....God prescribed every single detail of your body. He deliberately chose your race, the color of your skin, your hair, and every other feature. He also determined the natural talents you would possess and the uniqueness of your personality.[1]

God not only determines your DNA and your life purpose, the pivotal events of your life are also chosen by God. "It doesn't matter whether your parents were good or bad, or indifferent. God knew that those two individuals possessed exactly the right makeup to create a custom 'you' He had in mind."[2] In response to Warren's affirmation of God's choice of parents, a young man, recovering from years of family violence angrily objected, "It doesn't matter if your parents are good or bad – what's he talking about? It sure mattered in my life! What kind of God would choose two abusive drug addicts to be my parents? That's what a sadist would do. Not the loving God of Jesus Christ!" Warren doesn't shrink from the logical implications of divine sovereignty:

> "God has a purpose behind every problem, regardless of the cause, none of your problems could happen without God's permission. Everything that happens is Father-filtered even-

1    Rick Warren, *The Purpose Driven Life* (Grand Rapids, MI: Zondervan, 2002), 21, 22-23.
2    Ibid., 23.

when Satan or others meant it for bad....God's plan for your life includes all that happens to you – including your mistakes, your sins, your hurts. This includes illness, debt, disasters, divorce, and the death of loved ones."[1]

In these God-given and often challenging events, God is constantly testing us, seeing how we will respond to the good and bad fortune. Those who pass the test receive happiness in this life and a heavenly reward and thus justify, in Warren's mind, the challenges given to them. Those who fail God's tests will eventually fall into meaninglessness and miss out on God's promises of eternal life. But is the ultimate failure their own, or the failure of a god who can send us challenges but does not have the ability to help us respond to them in ways that bring salvation to wayward humanity?

At the end of the day, Warren must admit that God's love is conditional. Like the deity Job rails against, God is responsible for pain and death that are often too much for God's creatures to bear, spiritually, emotionally, relationally, and psychologically. Fallible and accident-prone humanity is left wondering if God is really on our side or if we are part of some cosmic experiment, and no more important to God than laboratory animals.

## Educating the Spirit

In the course of our childhoods, our parents place challenges in our lives to promote our emotional, ethical, and spiritual growth. Nearly every parent's heart breaks to hear her or his child crying as part of this learning process, such as learning to go to sleep on her or his own, walk to school by themselves, or face the consequences of bad decisions. Good parenting involves setting up prudent risks for our children. Parents insure the overall safety of their children by watching them closely at playgrounds or building fences around their yards, but a child who never scrapes her knee, falls off a bike, or hears the word "no" will never develop into a mature and responsible person.

---

1   Ibid., 194, 195-196.

The same dynamics apply to God's relationship with us. God does not create a perfect world, but an evolving world, with pockets of risk in every situation. God doesn't want us to stay spiritually and morally infantile but to grow toward holiness as a result of our own decisions as persons as members of communities. Philosopher John Hick described the challenges and free play of life, leading both to joy and sorrow in our lifetimes, as part of a "vale of soul making." In facing the challenges of life, we are able to grow in wisdom and stature and relationship with God. A world with freedom and creativity is risky, but the risks are worth it in terms of God's goal of spiritual maturity. Pain, suffering, and natural and moral evil are part of a good creation that promotes human spiritual growth and inspires courage and compassion.[1]

Yet, in real life, many persons don't respond successfully to the challenges of life or the inspirations to compassionate behavior. The impact of unjust and uncaring institutions, dysfunctional family situations, and our own physical and emotional limitations is just too great. Many are left by the wayside as a result of their own or others' decisions. This is the dilemma faced by Rick Warren's affirmation that the tests of life come from God's hand. If their lives are ultimately lost, either through missed possibilities or eternal damnation, then the problem of evil remains unsolved and God remains indictable for creating a world with so many failures. Eternal punishment for a misspent life reflects the possibility that God either lacks the love or power to save wayward humanity. In contrast, philosopher of religion John Hick believes that a loving and powerful God insures the eventual success and spiritual growth of all humanity. The reality of eternal life provides us with the opportunity to continue our spiritual growth and eventually experience our intended relationship with God. The education and spiritual role of pain is justified by God's ability to save all humankind and bring everyone to wholeness either in this life or the next.

Similar to this viewpoint is the Kabbalistic understanding of divine self-limitation or *tzitzum*, articulated by mystical teacher Isaac Luria and found in Harold Kushner's most recent reflec-

1   John Hick, *Evil and the God of Love* (New York: Harper and Row, 1966).

tions on Job. From this perspective, God's fullness would be an impediment to human freedom and creativity. Accordingly, God withdraws his full power so that creation has space to grow on its own. Divine self-limitation is the source of creativity and beauty and moral and natural evil. A world in which God did everything could be perfect: we would always make the right decisions, cells would follow their intended order, ticks would never carry Lyme disease, and earthquakes and storms would occur in uninhabited areas. But we would be entirely predictable and robotic in our perfection.

Divine withdrawal makes room for leviathan and behemoth to wreak havoc as well as to inspire awe. Divine withdrawal also creates space for raiders to steal Job's herds and storms to kill Job's children. Our calling in this risky universe is to become God's partners in *tikkun olam*, or healing the world. The problem of pain is solved by compassionate action toward those who suffer.[1]

## Saturday's Father

During the seventeenth and eighteenth centuries, the philosophy of Deism flourished among the intellectual communities of Europe and North America. Contrary to portrayals of the USA's founding fathers as Bible-believing Christians, most of the USA's first political leaders were heavily influenced by Deism, the belief that God establishes the laws of nature and then lets the universe unfold according to natural law, without any need for further divine intervention. God's activity is reserved to starting the cosmic process; after creation is established, God sits on the sidelines as an observer, refraining from any direct involvement in the pre-established harmony of divine law. Highly rational and scientific in their approach to the relationship of God and nature, the first Deists believed that divine wisdom did not require miracles or supernatural revelations to insure the well-being and spiritual education of humankind or the proper ordering of the universe.

---

1  Harold Kushner, *The Book of Job: When Bad Things Happen to a Good Person* (New York:Schocken, 2012).

Established by Divine Intelligence, the universe is governed by the inexorable laws of cause and effect. Freedom and chance exist within this divinely-established order. Earthquake and plague, cancer and moral evil, occur as a result of deviations from God's orderly universe and can be attributed to the native impact of human freedom and accidents of nature in this best of all possible worlds.

Deism encouraged humankind to take responsibility for its moral and scientific advancement. Like the philosophy of *tzitzum* of Jewish mysticism, it gave humankind the breathing space, denied by the all-determining God of Calvinism.

Deism, however, was not enough for many believers. They recognized the need for a god who was active in the ongoing affairs of persons and nations. While they accepted the inexorable and virtually unchanging laws of cause and effect, they affirmed the need for divine involvement in our lives, especially in answer to prayer and in rescue from calamity. Although God is outside the world, primarily as its first cause and moral observer, at specific times he "supernaturally" intervenes to change the course of nature. These miracles, supernatural violations of the laws of nature, occur to save God's chosen ones or in response to our ardent prayers. For example, I once heard a televangelist proclaim that if the Soviet Union attacked the USA with nuclear weapons, God will stretch out his mighty hand to deflect them. I have heard many televangelists assert that God will supernaturally cure cancer or provide you financial security in response to fervent prayer and financial donations!

Like a Saturday's father, God swoops in on the weekends with games, toys, trips to amusement parks, and fancy parties, while the everyday parent, usually a single mother, must deal with the ordinary domestic tasks that sustain the well-being of the children. God is content to let natural law unfold and will intervene if we do the proper rituals, for example, those prescribed by Job's friends, or if we pray fervently enough. Otherwise, we are at the mercy of inexorable cause and effect, established impersonally by God.

The problem with a miracle-making God for those who suffer is the reality that most people don't receive supernatural miracles in times of physical, emotional, economic, or relational duress. Was God, or our guardian angel, asleep at the switch when we needed them? Does God intervene only on behalf of some and not all? This miracle-minded God seldom intervenes supernaturally to halt most natural calamities, such as earthquakes and tsunami. Does this means that God cares only for some people and not others? Is God's bestowal of favor completely arbitrary? Or, perhaps, more challenging for the believer, is wondering if there a certain quantity or quality of prayer necessary to get God's attention and involvement in our lives.

On more than one occasion in my ministry, a parent or spouse has come to me, grieving the death of a loved one. He or she has felt abandoned by God. He or she has prayed, gone to church, made promises to God, and asked for the intercessions of the church, and yet their loved one died. This becomes especially heart-breaking when a neighbor simultaneously rejoices in God's supernatural involvement in bringing a loved one back from the brink of death. Often the bereaved parent or spouse wonders if a miracle did not occur because of lack of faith, the insufficiency of her or his prayers, or divine arbitrariness.

God's ways will always be mysterious to finite mortals. Yet, we still have a right to challenge theological doctrines that appear to arbitrarily favor some over others, or require certain moral, financial, or spiritual prerequisites to arouse God from inactivity.

## You Get What You Deserve

Civil order depends on proportionality between crime and punishment and effort and success. Every USA president promises a positive future to those who get an education, work hard, and play by the rules. Deep down, we believe that everyone should get what they deserve in this life or the next in terms of reward or punishment. The legal system and civil order requires some form of just deserts. Job's friends and much of Biblical tradition affirm that the good prosper and the evil suffer. Listen again to these words by Eliphaz:

*Think now, who that was innocent ever perished? Or where*
*were the upright cut off? As I have seen, those who plow iniquity*
*and sow trouble reap the same. By the breath of God they perish,*
*and by the blast of his anger they are consumed.* (4:7)

As singer-songwriter John Lennon once averred, "instant karma" connects joy and sorrow in our daily lives. The admonition "as
you sow so shall you reap" is at the heart of virtually every religious
tradition. Accordingly, the biblical tradition often saw illness as the
result of sin and good health as a reward for faithfulness to God.
The weakness of this position, as Job contends, is that the just often
suffer while robbers and thieves often prosper. Jesus challenged this
viewpoint as well. When he was asked whether a man's blindness
was the result of his or her parents' sin, Jesus responded with an
unequivocal "no." Jesus never gives a causal explanation for the
man's blindness but affirms that the healing will glorify God and
that the proper response to suffering is compassion, not analysis
or blame (John 9:1-7). Jesus doesn't sit around philosophizing but
takes the man aside, puts a poultice of mud and saliva on his eyes,
and heals him.

Neither Jesus, the author of Job, nor I dispute the fact that our
behaviors lead to consequences. The causal path, however, is often
circuitous and the result of many factors beyond our personal behavior or piety. The sun shines and rain falls on all people, regardless
of their moral state, as Jesus affirms (Matthew 5:45).

The doctrine of karma, originally found in Buddhist and Hin-
du philosophy, has become a popular explanation among many
North Americans for good and bad fortune over the past several
decades. Embracing both this life and our previous lifetimes, karma, action and reaction, are inexorable. We will reap what we sow
in this life or the next. The inequalities of birth are neither random
nor accidental but expressions of universal justice carrying over
from lifetime to lifetime.

In North America, the most popular understandings of karma are found among adherents of the new spiritual or new age
movements. Karma is invoked as an explanation, warning, and
educational tool. Just recently, at a local coffee house, I overheard

a couple baby boomers discussing a friend's string of bad luck. The first noted, "She sure is dealing with a lot of bad karma." Her companion mused humorously, "She must have been something awful in a past life." The new age approach of cause and effect states that everyone creates their own realities. From life to life, we create positive and negative events, reaping what we sow. The only way we can escape the wheel of karma is through spiritual insight and understanding the lessons we need to learn on our soul's journey. The current state of persons living in poverty or facing chronic illness is not unfair, but a working out of their personal destiny. While we can be compassionate toward them, it's their karma and they need to work it out on their own. At some level, this philosophy contends that we are all self-made individuals, journeying from life to life, creating good or bad fortune for ourselves based on our level of enlightenment and compassion toward others.

The acts-consequences approach to life, characteristic of Job's friends and the doctrine of karma, is profoundly fair, but it is also exacting and graceless. Whether the impact of our actions is meted out impersonally (karma) or by the rewards and punishments of a just God, there is little mercy in the process. A child born into poverty deserves her fate as a result of past life decisions; a woman diagnosed with cancer may connect the disease with youthful indiscretions; relatives mourning the deaths of children, parents, and spouses from an airline crash are told that all them are caught in a cycle of karmic justice.

Job's focus on real life experience is an important check on individualistic approaches that end up blaming the victim or congratulating the successful whether based on past or present life decisions. We are intricately connected in a fabric of relatedness. Poverty can't always be attributed to our personal decisions. Even the most dedicated and selfless workers, exhibiting the highest levels of personal integrity, are laid off when the plant closes and are impoverished in retirement by managerial financial misconduct. The most faithful parents sit hopelessly at the bedside of a dying child, whose illness is the result of living unbeknownst to them near a toxic dump site. While there may an undercurrent of providence that unconsciously guides our decisions, the nearly 3000 people who died as a result of terrorist attacks on September 11, 2001, were most likely a moral cross section of humanity, and no more deserving of their fate than the rest of us. Nor do I suspect that their spouses' or parents' moral flaws led to their tragic deaths.

## The Devil, You Say?

In the 1960's comedian Flip Wilson made a name for himself by invoking, "the Devil made me do it," to explain his misdeeds. Popular imagination and biblical theology attributes much of the pain and poor decision-making in life to diabolical sources. The gospels identify evil spirits as the source of physical and mental ill-ness. Like today's germ theory, the gospel writers believed demonic forces could invade a person's psyche, possessing her or his body, mind, and spirit. During his retreat in the wilderness, Jesus en-counters the Devil, who tempts him with food, power, and security. Throughout Christian history, Satan has been perceived by many to be the force of darkness and prince of this world, lying in wait to steal our souls or pervert our best intentions. To some Satan is a cosmic being, virtually equal in power to God, who will continue to wreak havoc on our planet until God's final victory, the Second Coming, in which the fallen order is destroyed and a new world, God's realm, is brought into existence.

While Job's ha-satan is an agent of God and not an evil spirit, the Hebraic scriptures/Old Testament also speak of a crafty demon-ic force, who brings death and destruction into the world by leading the original human couple to turn from God's vision for their lives. There may not have been an original *homo sapiens* couple; still, there are times when persons believe themselves to be possessed by powers greater than themselves, seeking to do them harm or lead them away from the good. In contrast to the all-good God, this perspective sees Satan is the father of lies, evil in every way. The belief in the existence of a satanic being has profound ethical and theological consequences. On the one hand, the craft and power of Satan tempts some people to abdicate responsibility for moral lapses that harm others. With Flip Wilson, they blame the prince of darkness for their peccadillos, claiming the "devil made me do it!" On the other hand, Satan's revolt against God and the image of Satan as a powerful counterforce to God suggests that God's power and intentionality is limited in power and impact. God is responsible only for the goodness of life, and cannot be invoked as a source of suffering. There is another "god," in this case, an evil one, who stands in the way of God's vision for the world and each of us. Yet, if Satan is one of God's creations who has gone astray, people are often left with no cosmic force who is unequivocally on their side: Satan is out to get them and God is always ready to punish them for their misdeeds or has a major role in causing the pain they experience!

## Stuff Happens

Many people believe the events of our lives are ultimately accidental. They see the universe and the processes of evolution that led to humankind and the growth of civilization as emerging from lucky and unlucky happenstances, competition between species, and the utter randomness of life. The universe simply unfolds without guidance and purpose. Given enough possibilities in the fourteen billion year journey of the universe, most of which end in failure, intelligent beings that can shape their daily lives and make plans for the future will emerge. An unplanned and purely accidental collision of asteroids may have led to one asteroid striking the earth, ending the age of dinosaurs, and making it possible for the human race to evolve over millions of years. Intelligence and purpose emerge, not through the influence of an Intelligent Being, but trial and error and competition for survival.

Over millennia, conscience and intellect emerged, but as noble as these are, they contribute to the long term survival value of the species and our particular communities and projects, not the emergence of an ethereal spirit. There is no god, no promised future, or ultimate fulfillment. Stuff simply happens in our blindly operating universe. The destruction of our species by an asteroid, a tidal wave that levels a city, or a proliferation of cancer cells that kills a young mother are accidents, neither no more nor less. We can reduce the risk factors for cancer or plan communities that insure greater safety in the event of a natural disaster. We can come together to respond to global climate change or the proliferation of nuclear arms. But, if we destroy ourselves or succumb to an incurable disease, there is no one ultimately to blame but us or the primitive state of our technology.

Compassion and ethics are possible in an utterly random universe. If nothing is promised or guaranteed, we can "eat, drink, and be merry, for tomorrow we die" or we can see our role as bringing beauty rather than ugliness to our momentary lives. We can nurture our children and children's children because their experiences and quality of life matter, even if this does not insure our community's survival value or nurture their spiritual lives. While Job and his friends believe that, for better or worse, our lives are shaped by divine power and intelligence, the voice in the whirlwind suggests that there are pockets of chaos in an essentially orderly universe. The randomness of the universe is a source of accidents, cancer cells, and tidal waves.

## What's Love Got to Do with It?

In his best-selling reflection on the problem of evil, Rabbi Harold Kushner asserted that the author of Job has had to choose between love and power. He believed in God's goodness and Job's goodness and was prepared to sacrifice an all-powerful God in favor of believing in the existence of a loving, moral God. In his interpretation of the voice from the whirlwind, Kushner suggests that divine creativity includes both order and chaos. God's descriptions of the interplay of cosmic order and creaturely wildness are intended to show Job that a perfectly running universe is impossible even for God. God can restrain the forces of chaos and disorder. God can place the stars in the sky and restrain the ocean tides, but sometimes asteroids hit the earth and on occasion the sea bursts its boundaries flooding dry land. The reality of free play and God's own interest in creaturely creativity opens the door to natural evils (tsunami, earthquake, and wind shear) as well as moral evils (political and personal injustice and violence). Job's punishment is not the result of God's choice, but the impact of a universe in which randomness and poor moral decision-making can disrupt God's intended order.[1]

Philosopher Alfred North Whitehead, the parent of process theology, asserts that "when the Western world accepted Christianity, Caesar conquered."[2] Power replaced love as the primary characteristic of God. Whitehead suggests that the image of God as a companion and guide provides an alternative to the divine apathy of Deism and the divine domination of John Calvin.

> There is, however, in the Galilean origin of Christianity another suggestion…. It does not empathize the ruling Caesar, or the ruthless moralist, or the unmoved mover. It dwells upon the tender elements in the world, which slowly and in quietness operate by love."[3]

Relationships rather than domination defines God's relationship to the world, according to Whitehead's vision of God. God's power is loving, rather than arbitrary. God works within the world, creating out of love, and bringing the best out of every situation. As one translation of Romans 8:28 asserts: "in all things, God works for good." God's power is relational rather than unilateral; God works in the context of real freedom and real creativity. Accordingly, evil and suffering do not primarily emerge as a result of divine decision-making, but from the interplay of multiple factors, ranging from environment, DNA, location, human choices, and environment to prayer and divine action. God is present in every situation, seeking the highest outcome, and although God's power is great, it always operates in relationship to the real world. God's power aims at goodness and creativity, but God must deal with

1 Harold Kushner, *When Bad Things Happen to Good People* (New York: Anchor, 1981).

2 Alfred North Whitehead, *Process and Reality: Corrected Edition* (New York: Free Press, 1978), 342.

3 Ibid., 343.

pockets of chaos at every level of existence from the molecular to the intergalactic.

As omnipresent, God influences all things. But God does not directly cause cancer or heart disease. In fact, there are times cancer cells appear to be more powerful than God. God does not desire the death of a recently married man or a mother in midlife from cancer. Still, God works within the reality of cancer to bring about health and well-being of body, mind, and spirit. Divine activity, not to mention ritual, prayer, and medicine, is not always successful in bringing about a cure, but God is always present as a force for wholeness and inspiration to compassion. God's power is displayed in the loving care of family members, the technical commitment and expertise of medical professionals, the energetic impact of complementary health care givers, and faithful friends. When there can't be a cure, there can still be a healing, a sense of calm acceptance, peace with God, and healing of relationships.

The ongoing processes of evolution, according to a relational understanding of power, integrate intentionality and randomness. God has a vision for the evolutionary process and every moment of our lives. God's vision is worked out in the context of natural selection, randomness, orderly causes, and creaturely creativity and freedom. God could have minimized human and non-human suffering by halting or slowing down the evolutionary process. Complexity of experience, characteristic of higher organisms, is connected with greater sensitivity to suffering of mind, body, spirit, and relationships as well as greater opportunity to cause pain and suffering by our moral decisions. Theologian David Ray Griffin affirms that "the freedom to enjoy a wide variety of bodily, moral, and religious values is also the freedom to make ourselves miserable....the same conditions that allow us to enjoy those experiences that we value most highly and would not [want] to live without are the conditions that lead us to suffer most intensely."[1] Further, the evolutionary process that brings forth higher organisms, like ourselves who can enjoy beauty and goodness, cherish relationships,

---

1    David Ray Griffin, *God, Power, and Evil: A Process Theodicy* (Louisville, KY: Westminster/John Knox, 2004), 292.

and create institutions, also leads to the existence of creatures that can wreak havoc in their environment.[1] Natural disasters often threaten our well-being because we build homes on earthquake faults and in the potential path of hurricanes and tornadoes. The tornado is amoral; our decisions had a role in putting us in harm's way. Our choices lead to both joy and sorrow, and God must deal creatively with the impact of our decisions by adapting God's vision to the pain we experience or cause.

In describing his evolving understanding of God from the perspective of a Nazi concentration camp, German theologian Dietrich Bonhoeffer proclaimed that only a suffering God can save. Seen solely in terms of unilateral power, the voice from the whirlwind, described by Job, shapes the world, but cannot fully empathize with human suffering. Worse yet, the god portrayed in the first two chapters of Job inflicts pain on innocent creatures, but does not personally feel consequences from the pain he has caused. Modeled after human sovereigns, God's perfection is seen in terms of action and not receptivity, power and not compassion. In contrast, a relational God experiences the world in its fullness, including its sorrow as well as joy. This is surely the meaning of the cross. God bears the burdens of his creativity and human sin. God feels all our pain, and does all that can be done to bring healing and redemption to the world.[2]

From the perspective of a relational, intimate, and compassionate God, the voice in the whirlwind is dialogical in nature. God hears Job's cries and feels Job's sense of abandonment. God did not sit idly by, observing dispassionately the death of Job's children. God experienced the terror of their last moments and the grief of Job and his wife. God may have inspired Job's protests against the order of the universe and quest for an image of God, more reflective of his own experience of pain and desolation. God's power is in the

1  Ibid., 394.

2  For more on this vision of reality, described by process theology, see Bruce Epperly, *Process Theology: Embracing Adventure with God* (Gonzales, FL: Energion Publications, 2014) and Bruce Epperly, *Process Theology: A Guide for the Perplexed* (London: T & T Clark, 2011).

movements of galaxies and solar systems, the order of the seasons, the restraint of the sea; God also moves through the compassion of loved ones and our own resilience in the face of tragedy. Suffering and pain are part of the fabric of life. We mortals are creatures of dust, and must all eventually face death and disease. Still, we are never alone. God is with us and nothing can separate us from the love of God.

The voice from the whirlwind is ultimately the breath of God's Spirit, urging forward the galaxies and planets, creatively bringing forth the non-human world in all its wonder and wildness, and inspiring human compassion, creativity, and questioning. The mighty winds of God move in all things, all creation is treasured by a heart whose compassion embraces the universe.

## Journeying with Job

In the spirit of the image of God's Spirit breathing through the whirlwind, take time to pause and experience God breathing in and through you. Close your eyes and begin to breathe slowly and gently. Feel your breath calming and energizing you. Let your breath spiritually center you. As you exhale, experience your connection with all creation in the intricate interdependence of life.

## Questions for Reflection

1) What aspect of God's nature can you most live without – God's ability to determine everything or God's desire to love everyone?

2) What do you think of Calvin's idea of divine determinism? What do you think of the idea of people being predestined to heaven and hell?

3) How would you evaluate the "educational" theory of pain and suffering? Can suffering help us grow? What happens to those who don't grow?

4) Do you believe that persons get what they deserve in this lifetime? What do you think of the doctrine of karma and its belief that our current situation is based on actions from

a previous lifetime? Does this encourage or discourage compassion?

5) Rick Warren states that God determines all the important events of your life without your input. Is this a helpful doctrine? How might it shape your behavior?

6) Isaac Luria and Harold Kushner speak of divine *tzitzum*, withdrawal or self-limitation to give humankind freedom and creativity. Why is *tzitzum* an important theological doctrine? Do you think God may have withdrawn too much for our own good?

7) How is the notion of supernatural miracles helpful to our faith? How is it problematic?

8) What do you think of the idea that things simply happen primarily by accident without any ultimate intentionality? Can a person be ethical in a random, godless world?

9) Does the devil make you do it? Do you believe in a literal devil? What are the benefits from believing in a satanic figure? What are the problems of holding this belief?

10) How do you evaluate a God who must work within the events of life, adapting to the creativity of the world, rather than determining events from the outside? Is the goodness and love of God strong enough to be of help to us?

11) What do you think of an empathetic, suffering God? Is this helpful in responding to your suffering?

# 7 PRAYER IN AN UNCERTAIN UNIVERSE

*O*nce upon a time, Job believed that saying the right kind of prayers guaranteed that you and your loved ones would be blessed. When life was going well, Job, playing his role as the dutiful parent sought to protect his partying children from divine punishment by rising early in the morning and offering burnt offerings for each child. He saw religious ritual as a type of barter between God and himself, insuring success and minimizing failure for himself and his loved ones.

When Job falls on hard times, his friends prescribe exactly the same rituals as a remedy for his sin and suffering. Bildad advises, "If you will seek God and make supplication to the Almighty, if you are pure and upright, surely then he will rouse himself for you and restore you to your rightful place" (9:6). Zophar adds, "if you direct your heart rightly, you will stretch out your hands toward him…. You will be secure, and will not fear. You will forget your misery… And your life will be brighter than the noonday. Its darkness will be like the morning" (11:13, 16-17).

Job and his friends believe that if you have the right formula, your prayers will be answered and you will enjoy personal well-being and financial prosperity. Lack of faith and poorly executed rituals will lead, in contrast, to sickness and poverty. One of Job's friends even suggests that just such a moral and liturgical lapse may have contributed to the death of Job's children. Our prayers make all the difference in the world. If you get it right, you are blessed.

If you forget to pray or don't pray in the right way, you and your loved ones will suffer!

## The Perils of the Prosperity Gospel

Today, many Christians follow variations of what has been described as the prosperity gospel. According to this viewpoint, there is a seamless relationship between the physical and spiritual realms. Created in God's image, we can have dominion over the physical world, including our health and financial situation. If you have enough faith, God will give you anything you want, even to the extent of suspending the regular and predicable relationships of cause and effect. Wealth reflects God's blessing, grounded in our faithfulness to God and our positive confession God's dominion over the world. Poverty is the result of curses put in motion by our lack of faith and failure to tap into God's laws of prosperity. God has covenanted through scripture to set up a contract in which God will fulfill God's promises to all who believe and plant seeds of prosperity, especially through their generosity to prosperity-oriented ministries. This is the religious barter system in its most crass and materialistic form.

Despite God's command that Job perform sacrifices to absolve his friend's guilt, the poetic sections of Job challenge any linear acts-consequences transactional relationship between God and humankind. Non-religious people can live in opulence while faithful followers of God are plunged into poverty. Proper execution of rituals may make a difference, but they don't guarantee good fortune for us or our offspring.

## The Problems of Positive Thinking

Similar in tone to the prosperity gospel is, ironically, the use of affirmations and positive visualization by proponents of new spiritual, new thought, mind cure, and new age philosophies. The most recent exposition of the power of the mind to transform reality in a linear, belief-consequences approach is Rhonda Byrne's

*The Secret.* The message of *The Secret* is simple – persons can create whatever they want in life through positive self-talk and visualization exercises. According to Byrne, the secret of life can be described in terms of the one basic and immutable law of the universe, "the law of attraction," by which our positive and negative thoughts will eventually become manifest in the circumstances of our lives. Byrne promises success to anyone who applies *The Secret* to her or his life: positive thinking and visualization can give you whatever you want.[1]

Through the law of attraction, we can literally create our own realities. This can be liberating; and it can also lead to guilt and alienation. If our lives are an exact reflection of our thought processes, as *The Secret* asserts, then poverty, violence, abuse, and disenfranchisement, are primarily the result of holding onto negative images of our lives and the world and not interpersonal, economic, and social structures of alienation and injustice. We attract everything that happens to us by the quality of our thinking and attitudes. Those who suffer must have done something to deserve their cancer or poverty. The impact of social injustice and discrimination must ultimately be the result of our individual negativity and not unjust social structures, requiring social and political remedies. This can be spiritually devastating, but, as Byrne asserts, it also can be life-transforming. If we change our consciousness, Byrne believes, our world will immediately change as well.

The solution to poverty and illness, given by the prosperity gospel and new age pundits, is virtually the same as that of Job's friends. Turn to God, make a confession of faith, visualize prosperity and success, banish negative thinking, and your life will turn around. This is great advice when life is joyful and your needs are being met. But this positive vision is bought at the price of blaming victims of disease, injustice, poverty, and accident for their predicaments. The quest for a completely orderly universe in which rewards and punishments are proportional, may lead to both blaming those who suffer for their suffering and neglecting to change the social forces that lead to poverty, ill-health, and alienation.

1   Rhonda Byrne, *The Secret* (Atria Books, 2006)

## Prayer in an Uncertain World

Throughout her life, my mother experienced depression, obsessional thinking, and low self-esteem. She received electroshock treatments in the late 1950's when the darkness of depression overwhelmed her emotional and spiritual life. Every day was difficult for her, yet she was a person of faith, and a dedicated early childhood educator, despite all the trials she faced. She believed in the power of prayer and holding fast to God's promises in scripture, embodied in the magnetic plaque that greeted me whenever I opened our refrigerator, *Prayer Changes Things*. I believe that the tried and tested Job would have appreciated her understanding of prayer. Prayer is not a panacea but a practice that makes a way when there is no way, and enables us to go through the darkest valley, with wild beasts all around, trusting that God is with us.

Jesus makes some bold statements about prayer. He proclaims: "Ask and it will be given you; search, and you will find; knock, and the door will be opened for you" (Matthew 7:7). He promised that his followers can do "greater things" than they can imagine in living out the gospel (John 14:12). He believed that even a little faith can move mountains (Matthew 17:20).

Jesus promised great things, but recognized that life gives us no guarantees. Jesus believed that God "makes the sun rise on the evil and the good, and sends rain on the righteous and the unrighteous" (Matthew 5:45). Recognizing that resurrection emerges from the transformation of suffering, Jesus promises that those who follow him will receive great things in a world of uncertainty:

> *Truly, I tell you, there is no one who has left house or brothers or sisters or mother or father or children or fields, for my sake and the sake of the good news, who will not receive a hundredfold now in this age – houses, brothers and sisters, mothers and children, and fields, with persecutions – and in the age to come eternal life.* (Mark 10:29-30)

Great joy, but also persecutions! Following God, and a life of prayer, may lead to suffering. But amid and beyond the suffering, we can experience the blessings of a relationship with God. Suffering comes to all, and within our suffering and persecution, we will discover God's loving presence, enabling us to face what we can't change with grace and dignity.

Job doesn't give us a theology of prayer. He gives us an example of a life saturated by prayerful relatedness to God. Even in his anger and desolation, his sense of abandonment, Job takes everything, even his protests, to God in prayer.

In light of Job's experiences, how shall we understand the power of prayer to transform our lives? Prayer makes a difference. In fact, scientific studies connect prayer with improved health outcomes. In examining the medical research on the power of prayer, Larry Dossey affirms that prayer is good medicine. Based on scores of medical studies that associate religious activities with better health, longer lives, and greater life satisfaction, another physician, Harold Koenig proclaims that religion is good for your health.[1]

Job would not challenge these medical findings but he would warn us not to assume a linear cause and effect relationship between prayer and good health and positive thinking and personal success. Prayer transforms our lives, but prayer is but one factor in our health and well-being. Prayer connects us with God and a deeper relationship with God may mean letting go of success, comfort, safety, and security. Prayer involves aligning ourselves with God's vision and not demanding that God's vision conform to our desires or interests. God wants to bless us, and God wants to bless all of us in a world in which the well-being of all is more important than individual success and self-interest. The problem with the prosperity gospel and new age formulae for creating your own reality is that they focus on our individual well-being and forget the global context of our lives.

When we say "your will be done," an essential component of a healthy spiritual life, we place our interests in a broader perspec-

1  Larry Dossey, *Prayer is Good Medicine* (New York: Harper One, 1997), Harold Koenig, *The Healing Power of Faith* (New York: Simon and Schuster, 2001); Dale Matthews, *The Faith Factor: The Proof of the Healing Power of Prayer* (New York: Penguin, 1999).

tive than our individual desires. We grow in wisdom and stature and discover that the well-being of others and the planet are often more important than our own individual prosperity. God's will is moral, and not all-determining; it presents us with visions of what life can be like and then inspires us to seek the best possible world for ourselves and others.

Job experiences peace when he sees his whole life, and even his suffering, in light of the wondrous tragic beauty of God's creation, which is both dynamic and orderly, and wild and chaotic, and everywhere reflecting the creative wisdom of God. Job discovers that God's creative wisdom, reflected in the orderly and dependable movements of the universe, provides the undergirding for a meaningful life, and that within this order are elements of chaos and unpredictability. Moreover, the very characteristics of divine creativity that provide the order necessary for abundant life – gravity, predictable cause and effect relationships, physical pain as a warning signal – can be sources of injury and distress.

## Prayer Without Guarantees

In a universe characterized by inexorable forms of order as well as free play, novelty, and pockets of chaos, prayer can be a tipping point between life and death, health and illness, and success and failure. Prayer takes us beyond ourselves to seek the well-being of our loved ones and people we'll never meet. In an interdependent universe, reflective of Job's mystical vision, prayer is one factor among many in every situation. Our prayers make a difference and shape the future of our loved ones and institutions necessary for civil order and creativity. In ways we cannot imagine, our prayers radiate across the universe, without regard to space or time, opening the door to positive outcomes for those for whom we pray and ourselves. They create a positive field of force that transforms the circumstances of life. Our prayers are woven by God into the fabric of the universe and the situations for which we pray along with the impact of past events and decisions, the current health, economic, or relational situation, DNA and cultural history, the prayers of others, the non-human-environment, and many other factors beyond our knowledge or control. Prayer can tip the scales, awaken new possibilities, transform character, give new hope, give birth to quantum leaps of energy that change cells and souls, and slow the progress of incurable disease. Each morning I pray for my grandchildren, wife, son and daughter-in-law, congregation, and a dear friend. I believe that my prayers have and continue to make a difference in their lives. I believe my prayers add to their happiness and improve their health conditions. Yet, I also know from sad experience that my prayers do not guarantee cures and changes in life circumstances. Still, I pray because it connects us in a circle of love.

The same many-faceted relationship of cause and effect applies to our faith, use of positive affirmations, and spiritual visualizations, all of which can be medically described as forms of the placebo effect. What we believe can transform our lives and can lead to positive events in our health, professional lives, relationships, and spirituality. To some extent, our beliefs shape our biology and our interpretations of life events, opening or closing the door to new energies promoting our well-being and the health of others. The problem with the prosperity gospel and some forms of new age spirituality is that they assume we can liberate ourselves from predictable cause and effect relationships as well as the impact of the social and interpersonal environment on our well-being. They assert that if we have faith, we will automatically succeed. If we visualize a particular outcome, it will automatically occur to our benefit or detriment. In contrast, I believe that faith matters, but faith like prayer is always contextual and needs to be placed in the context of God's vision for us and the world and our own personal and environmental realities.

It is important to remember that although God's beloved messenger and savior Jesus could bring about remarkable and miraculous transformations of body, mind, spirit, and nature, Jesus' own power was limited and shaped by his environment. Ponder a moment this passage describing Jesus' own limitations:

*And they [the citizens of Jesus' hometown Nazareth] took*
*offense at him. Then Jesus said to them, "Prophets are not without*
*honor, except in their own hometown, and among their own kin,*
*and their own house." And he could do no deed of power there,*
*except that he laid his hands on a few sick people and cured them.*
*And he was amazed at their unbelief.* (Mark 6:4-6)

Jesus was limited by his spiritual environment: faith opened the door to healing energy; unbelief blocked Jesus' healing power. Without going into great detail, the biblical narrative describes a dynamic call and response in which humans are free to say "yes" or "no" to God's call to wholeness. God often has to adjust his actions to our belief or unbelief, adapting God's ways to open us to his dream for our lives and the world.

Perhaps the greatest gift of prayer is the recognition that even if there isn't a cure there can be a healing. We can experience God's nearness regardless of life's circumstances. This is the heart of the *Serenity Prayer*, attributed to theologian Reinhold Niebuhr. The *Serenity Prayer* recognizes our weakness and limitation, and affirms that personal transformation that may occur when we place our present and future in God's care one moment at a time. This is good news not only for persons with addictions but for all of us who face the physical, emotional, intellectual, and spiritual limits inherent in our mortality and in a world of accident and wonder alike.

> *God, grant me the serenity to accept the things I cannot change,*
> *The courage to change the things I can,*
> *And wisdom to know the difference.*

Niebuhr's longer version, first appearing in print in 1951, places our lives in a wider perspective in which the healing of emotions and spiritual transformation occur when we place our lives in God's hands, trusting God's wisdom to guide our path and God's presence to bring peace in circumstances that may never change – the realities of addiction, incurable and chronic illness, the impact of accident and others' harmful decisions.

*God, give me grace to accept with serenity*
*to accept the things that cannot be changed,*
*Courage to change the things*
*which should be changed,*
*and the Wisdom to distinguish*
*the one from the other.*
*Living one day at a time,*
*Enjoying one moment at a time,*
*Accepting hardship as a pathway to peace,*
*Taking, as Jesus did,*
*This sinful world as it is,*
*Not as I would have it,*
*Trusting that You will make all things right,*
*If I surrender to Your will,*
*So that I may be reasonably happy in this life,*
*And supremely happy with You forever in the next.*
*Amen.*

Perhaps my mother was right. In an uncertain world, prayer changes things and faith gives us the courage to gratefully and lovingly endure what cannot be changed. My mother daily dealt with her own personal demons. She did not expect them to disappear; but she trusted that God would give her the wisdom and power to respond to every need and that his grace was sufficient for her and the sons for whom she prayed.

The book of Job ends with the affirmation that Job's good life included his mortality. The message of Job is that our spiritual commitments and faith in God gives us courage to face what cannot be changed, the confidence to challenge our images of God, and the willingness to stay in relationship with God even when God seems absent. In the experience of suffering, we may become embittered. We may also discover that God feels our pain and provides us a pathway through the wilderness and mighty winds to propel us forward. In facing suffering with God, we may discover our inner freedom to choose our responses to what can't be changed and become God's partners in changing what is in our power in God's quest to heal the world.

## Journeying with Job

Pause several times today to give thanks for the wonders of life and your own life situation. Consider all the gifts that you have received and that allow you to experience beauty, love, and responsibility. Amid your gratitude, consider those for whom you are called to pray. Quietly visualize these persons or life situations as you commit each to God's care. Trust that God is working in these persons and situations to bring about something of beauty.

## Questions for Reflection

1) In what ways are the prosperity gospel and some new age philosophies similar? What do you think of the notion that our faith and positive thinking can create our own realities? What happens when we are failures at achieving our goals or God's plan for our lives?

2) "Turn to God, make a confession of faith, visualize prosperity and success, banish negative thinking, and your life will turn around." How do you evaluate that statement? In what ways might it be true? In what ways is it spiritually dangerous?

3) How do you understand this statement of Jesus? How does it relate to our understanding of suffering and pain? "Ask and it will be given you; search, and you will find; knock, and the door will be opened for you." (Matthew 7:7)

4) Read Mark 10:29-30. How do you understand the juxtaposition of blessing and persecution? In what ways might persecution be part of a good life, seen as a whole? Is success always the sign of God's blessing?

5) What do you think of the growing evidence that religion is good for a person's health? In what ways might the faith-health connection contribute to spiritual growth? In what ways might it create problems for faith communities?

6) Do you regularly pray? How would you characterize your prayer style? For what do you pray? Do you think your prayers make a difference? If so, how much of a difference do they make?

7) What do you think of the notion that prayer can be a tipping point, though not the only factor, between health and illness, and success and failure?

8) What does it mean to say "when there can't be a cure, there can be a healing"? Do you believe that people can experience healing even if their personal situation remains painful?

9) What aspect of the complete *Serenity Prayer* is most inspiring to you?

10) What is your role as God's companion in healing the world? Do your actions make a difference in the future of others and the planet? Can your faithfulness be a tipping point between health and illness, and positive and negative outcomes?

# FOR FURTHER JOURNEYS WITH JOB

I have found the following books helpful in my own journeys with Job:

Epperly, Bruce. *Process Theology: Embracing Adventure with* God. (Gonzalez, FL, Energion, 2014).

_____. *Process Theology: A Guide for the Perplexed.* (London: T&T Clark, 2011).

_____. *Emerging Process: Adventurous Theology for a Missional Church.* (Cleveland, TN, Parson's Porch Books, 2012).

Fretheim, Terence. *Creation Untamed: The Bible, God, and Natural Disasters* (Ada. MI: Baker, 2010).

Kushner, Harold. Harold Kushner, *The Book of Job: When Bad Things Happen to a Good Person* (New York: Schocken, 2012).

_____. *When Bad Things Happen to Good People.* (New York: Anchor, 1981).

Lewis, C.S. *The Problem of Pain.* (New York: HarperCollins, 2009).

Melchert, Charles. *The Book of Job* (Lancaster, PA: Lancaster Theological Seminary Office of Continuing Education, 2007).

Mitchell, Stephen. *The Book of Job.* (New York: Harper, 1979).

Newsom, Carol. *The Book of Job: A Contest of Moral Imagination.* (New York: Oxford University Press, 2003).

Rohr, Richard. *Job and the Mystery of Suffering.* (New York: Crossroad, 1996).

Tillich, Paul. *The Courage to Be.* (New Haven: Yale University Press, 2000).

_____. *The Dynamics of Faith.* )New York: Harper Brothers, 1958).

## ALSO FROM ENERGION PUBLICATIONS

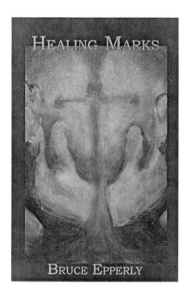

… inspirational, timely, insightful, and wise.

**Edwin David Aponte**
Christian Theological Seminary

Bruce has given us an excellent translation/introduction to this important theological movement that is drawing the attention of many who once wrote it off as "unpreachable!"

**Robert D. Cornwall, PhD**
Pastor

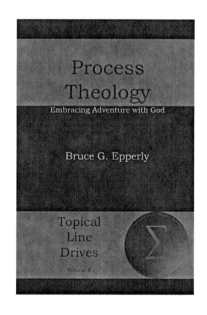

# MORE FROM ENERGION PUBLICATIONS

## Personal Study
| | | |
|---|---|---|
| Holy Smoke! Unholy Fire | Bob McKibben | $14.99 |
| The Jesus Paradigm | David Alan Black | $17.99 |
| When People Speak for God | Henry Neufeld | $17.99 |
| The Sacred Journey | Chris Surber | $11.99 |

## Christian Living
| | | |
|---|---|---|
| It's All Greek to Me | David Alan Black | $3.99 |
| Grief: Finding the Candle of Light | Jody Neufeld | $8.99 |
| My Life Story | Becky Lynn Black | $14.99 |
| Crossing the Street | Robert LaRochelle | $16.99 |
| Life as Pilgrimage | David Moffett-Moore | 14.99 |

## Bible Study
| | | |
|---|---|---|
| Learning and Living Scripture | Lentz/Neufeld | $12.99 |
| From Inspiration to Understanding | Edward W. H. Vick | $24.99 |
| Philippians: A Participatory Study Guide | Bruce Epperly | $9.99 |
| Ephesians: A Participatory Study Guide | Robert D. Cornwall | $9.99 |
| Ecclesiastes: A Participatory Study Guide | Russell Meek | $9.99 |

## Theology
| | | |
|---|---|---|
| Creation in Scripture | Herold Weiss | $12.99 |
| Creation: the Christian Doctrine | Edward W. H. Vick | $12.99 |
| The Politics of Witness | Allan R. Bevere | $9.99 |
| Ultimate Allegiance | Robert D. Cornwall | $9.99 |
| History and Christian Faith | Edward W. H. Vick | $9.99 |
| The Journey to the Undiscovered Country | William Powell Tuck | $9.99 |
| Process Theology | Bruce G. Epperly | $4.99 |

## Ministry
| | | |
|---|---|---|
| Clergy Table Talk | Kent Ira Groff | $9.99 |
| Out of This World | Darren McClellan | $24.99 |

Generous Quantity Discounts Available
Dealer Inquiries Welcome
Energion Publications — P.O. Box 841
Gonzalez, FL_ 32560
Website: http://energionpubs.com
Phone: (850) 525-3916

CPSIA information can be obtained
at www.ICGtesting.com
Printed in the USA
LVOW08s2352020118
561516LV00001BA/56/P

9 781631 991073